DERAILING DEMOCRACY

The America the Media
Don't Want You to See

David McGowan

Not Your Parents' Harper's *Index*

Common Courage Press   Monroe, ME

Library of Congress Cataloging-in-Publication Data

McGowan, David, 1960-
    Derailing Democracy : the America the media don't
want you to see / David McGowan.
        p. cm.
    Includes bibliographical references and index.
    ISBN 1-56751-184-8 (pbk.) -- ISBN 1-56751-185-6
(cloth)
        1. Social problems--United States--Miscellanea.
    2. United States--Social conditions--1980--Miscellanea.
    3. United States--Politics and government--1989--
Miscellanea. I. Title.

HN59.2.M424 2000
361.1'0973
                                                                99-054185

Common Courage Press
PO Box 702
Monroe, ME 04951

(207) 525-0900; fax: (207) 525-3068
orders-info@commoncouragepress.com

www.commoncouragepress.com

First Printing

*To Alissa, Megan and Shane, in the hope that
we might begin to build a better world for them.
And to Gretchen, for her unwavering support and
limitless patience through long periods of neglect.*

The U.S.A. has been quick to voice its condemnation of human rights violations in some other countries and to stress, by contrast, the wealth of civil and political rights which it guarantees within its borders...however, it has failed to deliver these rights to many of its people and there are signs that, **unless urgent steps are taken,** *these rights will be further eroded...It is with a sense of urgency, therefore, that Amnesty International is launching a major campaign on human rights violations in the U.S.A.*

— Amnesty International

We are not afraid to entrust the American people with unpleasant facts, foreign ideas, alien philosophies, and competitive values. For a nation that is afraid to let its people judge the truth and falsehood in an open market is a nation that is afraid of its people.

— President John Fitzgerald Kennedy

How fortunate for governments that the people they administer don't think.

— Adolph Hitler

Contents

Introduction

*I know of no country in which there is so little independence
of mind and real freedom of discussion as in America.*

— **Alexis de Tocqueville (1805–1859)**

It has been almost 40 years since President Eisenhower, in his final address to the nation before leaving office in 1961, issued a rather extraordinary warning to the American people that the country "must guard against unwarranted influence, whether sought or unsought, by the military-industrial complex. The potential for the disastrous rise of misplaced power exists and will persist." Tragically, Eisenhower's warning was not heeded, and the beast has been allowed not only to grow, but to mutate into something that should more accurately be referred to as the military-industrial-media complex.

Following the same course that virtually every other major industry has in the last two decades, a relentless series of mergers and corporate takeovers has consolidated control of the media into the hands of a few corporate behemoths. The result has been that an increasingly authoritarian agenda has been sold to the American people by a massive, multi-tentacled media machine that has become, for all intents and purposes, a propaganda organ of the state.

It is precisely because most readers get their news filtered through that same organ that many will readily disagree with this assessment. The American free press is the envy of the world, they

1

will argue, and this unprecedented ability that we as Americans have to enjoy unrestricted access to unfiltered news is one of the unique freedoms that makes America the icon of democratic ideals that we all know it to be. And it is certainly true that by all outward appearances the United States does appear to have the very epitome of a free press.

After all, do not CNN and a handful of would-be contenders broadcast a continuous stream of news to America's millions of cable subscribers? Are Tom Brokaw, Peter Jennings, Dan Rather and Ted Koppel, as well as countless lesser-knowns, not welcomed into our homes nightly, bearing the day's news—both good and bad? Would not our morning rituals seem woefully lacking without the comfort of the morning paper on the breakfast table? And don't the radio waves crackle incessantly with the political musings of Rush Limbaugh and his legions of ideological clones, while a bustling "alternative" press brings the "progressive" version of news and events to those of a slightly different political persuasion? Miss something during the week? Not to worry: *Time, Newsweek* or *U.S. News and World Report* are there with a handy weekly round-up of the big stories. Don't have time to read? No problem: *60 Minutes, 20/20, 48 Hours* and *Dateline NBC* have already read them for you— just sit back and mainline the week's events.

Yet behind this picture of plurality there are clear warning signs that an increasingly incestuous relationship exists between the media titans and the corporate military powers that Eisenhower so feared. For example, the number-one purveyor of broadcast news in this country—NBC, with both MSNBC and CNBC under its wing, as well as NBC news and a variety of "newsmagazines"—is now owned and controlled by General Electric, one of the nation's largest defense contractors. Is it not significant that as GE's various media subsidiaries predictably lined up to cheerlead the use of U.S. military force in Kosovo, it was at the same time posting substantial profits from the sale of the high tech tools of modern warfare it so shamelessly glorifies?

Would we not loudly condemn such a press arrangement were it to occur in a nation such as Russia or China? Equally alarming is that those viewers choosing to change channels to CNN, the reigning king of the cable news titans, were treated to the surreal daily spectacle of watching Christiane Amanpour, who is the wife of State Department mouthpiece James Rubin, analyze her husband's daily press briefings, as though she could objectively respond to the mounds of disinformation spewing forth from the man with whom she shares her morning coffee. Were it to occur elsewhere, would this not be denounced as symptomatic of a state-run press?

Maybe. Yet it can still be argued that corporate media owner-ship, despite the ominous implications, does not necessarily pre-clude the notion of a free press in that ownership has little to do with the day-to-day functioning of the news media. After all, one could reasonably argue, the press operates on the principle of com-petition to break the big story, and if one news outlet is reticent to report unfavorably on its owners or the government, surely it risks being beaten by competitors. We all know that ambitious reporters are driven by an obsessive desire to get "the scoop." Does not the mere existence of literally thousands of print and broadcast news sources, all keeping their eyes on the Pulitzer Prize, provide *ipso facto* proof of a free press? Does it not guarantee that all the news that merits reporting will arrive on our doorstep each morning in a rela-tively objective form?

This is a perfectly logical argument, yet there is substantial evi-dence that suggests that competition does not in itself overcome the interests of the corporate media. For example, while saturation cov-erage is given to such non-news events as the premier of a new *Star Wars* movie, there has not been a single American media source reportimg the fact that the first successful human clones have been created, despite the staggering implications of such a scientific mile-stone. Surely a press motivated by competition to break the big story would have stumbled upon this one by now, especially considering that as of this writing, more than a year has passed since the world was blessed with the first human clone, courtesy of an American biotechnology firm. (See Chapter 12)

Of course, this could be due not to media suppression, but to the simple fact that the press failed to uncover this story. However, this interpretation fails to account for the fact that this is far from being the only newsworthy event that the American media have failed to take note of, as evidenced throughout this book. It also fails to explain why the British press seem to have had little trouble unearthing this particular story, or why the U.S. news media continued to ignore the issue even after it had appeared in print in the U.K. Had this story been aired by our own press corps, it surely would have received an overwhelmingly negative response. This is, no doubt, the very reason that this story, as well as countless others, has failed to make its American debut.

Yet the illusion of a free and competitive press persists and has become ingrained to the point that it is nearly universally accepted as a truism. And with it comes the illusion that America's people are among the world's best informed. If not, then it is surely our own fault for being too lazy or otherwise preoccupied to avail ourselves of the media barrage. *Politically Incorrect*'s Bill Maher can be heard regularly haranguing guests for failing to utilize these readily-available resources to gain an informed knowledge of the issues, occasionally even offering up the opinion that anyone who has failed to do so should be stripped of the right to vote. Maher is only stating outright what is implied in the message of the media in general: the truth is right here before your eyes—you have only to partake to become an informed citizen.

But the "truth" offered by the media is a systematic and deliberate distortion of reality. In some cases, such as the previously cited example of human cloning, this distortion takes the form of outright suppression. In many other cases, it takes the form of distraction, never more prominently on display than during the O.J. Simpson media circus. The coverage afforded this case, and others such as the JonBenet Ramsey case, while creating the illusion that the press is examining the seamy underbelly of American society, does little to shed light on the very real problems facing the average American. These stories, as well as the countless tales of individual human failing that spring forth from the media fascination with the cult of celebrity, are clearly not meant to inform, but to distract and entertain.

Sometimes something far more insidious is at play than mere distraction, however. By far the most dangerous form of distortion, and one that has become increasingly prominent, involves the willful misrepresentation of issues in such a way that the "debate" on the issue then begs solutions that actually exacerbate the real problem that was being masked. In this way, problems that are themselves borne of the increasingly reactionary agenda being pursued are perceived to be solved by resorting to yet further erosion of democratic and civil rights.

One example where this phenomenon can be seen at work is in the media coverage of school shootings. Following each such incident, a pseudo debate is conducted in which the blame is variously placed on guns, rock/rap music, or video games as the cause in the rise in "youth violence." The debate is restricted to these now familiar parameters. But behind the sensational headlines, the media fail to note that youth violence has actually declined, and that these incidents are not a uniquely adolescent phenomenon, but are in fact patterned after the acts of adults, with the high school serving as the teenage equivalent of the post office or the day trading center.

The problem, viewed in a larger context, is not with the current generation of kids, but with society as a whole. The fact that Americans of all ages choose to strike out violently against society and its institutions, however infrequently, is a clear warning sign of a pronounced decay in America's social fabric. Why does the current social system, purportedly the very model of freedom and justice, breed such extreme levels of anger, frustration and despair, as well as the willingness to express these feelings in such explosive outbursts? This question is outside the media's scope.

Neither is it questioned why all of society, including our youth, is bombarded from literally all directions with the message that the use of force is an effective, and even desirable, means of achieving one's goals, and that pity and compassion for others is a sign of weakness. This message is certainly not confined to pop culture and the entertainment media.

Virtually the same message is conveyed by America's increasing reliance on brute force as an instrument of foreign policy and by the shameless glorification of U.S. military prowess. It is conveyed as well by the increasingly militarized tactics of the nation's police, most recently visible in the heavy-handed approach of the Seattle police towards the tens of thousands of overwhelmingly peaceful protestors at the December 1999 conference of the World Trade

Organization. It is further reinforced by Congress each time it drafts a new round of "law and order" legislation, and by the increasingly free rein given the nation's police and correctional officers to enforce those laws.

Rather than acknowledge any of this, each school shooting will be propagandized for its fear-inducing value, with the same script being played out, leading to the same preordained solution: while repeating the mantra that "we will never be able to fully understand why these things occur" (which is certainly true if we don't ask the right questions), yet another round of reactionary sentencing legislation will be passed with additional laws designed to criminalize our children. Far from solving the underlying problems and social tensions, all such legislation will ultimately serve only to foster increased feelings of anger, resentment and hopelessness.

This is but one example of how a handful of key media players determine what the "issues" are and what the parameters of public debate on those issues will be by controlling both the flow and the shape of the news. When a problem is identified, it is defined in the narrowest of contexts so as to preempt any discussion outside of the pre-defined boundaries—any argument put forth outside of those boundaries can then be mocked or ignored. In this way, anything remotely resembling an informed public debate on the serious issues facing this country is effectively cut off.

Instead, what we have is artificially truncated debate, usually by a relentless procession of allegedly politically informed pundits clustering into various formations to populate the cable news talk shows, where the rapid fire verbiage can almost obscure the fact that nothing of relevance is actually being said. These programs, and the broadcast media in general, are not meant to enlighten; they are intended to provide a pre-packaged debate, presenting the acceptable arguments for both sides. At the same time, they are meant to entertain and distract attention away from whatever essential information is being withheld from the discussion.

An informed populace is a critical component of any truly democratic system, and a nation that has only the illusion of public debate has no more than the illusion of democracy as well. That is why it is absolutely crucial that the people of America have full access to all the information that affects their lives as citizens of this country, and of the world community. As an effort towards achieving that goal, presented here you will find some of the news that wasn't quite fit to print.

A brief discussion on sources, credibility and context is warranted here. The source material for this book falls into one of five general categories:

- U.S. government documents and statements by U.S. officials
- Documents and reports issued by Non-Governmental Organizations (NGOs), such as Amnesty International and the Justice Policy Institute
- "Mainstream" media sources, e.g. the *Los Angeles Times* and the *New York Times*
- "Alternative" media sources, including *The Nation* and *The Mojo Wire* (the electronic version of *Mother Jones*)
- The foreign press, such as the *London Times* and Australia's *The Age*

Of these five, official government documents were considered the most credible, and were therefore the most sought after. This is certainly not to suggest that the various branches of the U.S. government are noted for their honesty. On the contrary, lying is an integral element of the business of government, not only in America but around the world. However, government disinformation tends to follow a fairly steady pattern, namely casting the purveyor of the propaganda in the best possible light.

Given that the documents excerpted here tend, to the contrary, to damage America's carefully crafted public image, they were deemed to be the most credible and therefore the most difficult to refute. The other primary source of documents was from NGOs, which were considered to be somewhat less credible due to the obvious fact that all such organizations have a political agenda, leaving them open to charges of bias. It is notable, however, that the media generally finds the information released by these entities quite credible when it casts America in a positive light, carefully sidestepping the more unsavory facts, issues and trends.

The balance of the material presented here was culled from the various newsmedia sources listed above. Whenever possible, what are generally considered to be mainstream sources were consulted first, beginning with the largest and most influential of the major daily newspapers. In those cases where the mainstream media failed to yield the desired information, the alternative media was next utilized. As a last resort, the foreign press was turned to on those issues which drop completely off the American media's radar screen.

And why, given that a central argument thus far has been that the function of the media is to obscure rather than to inform, should any credence be given to these sources? For the simple reason that occasionally bits and pieces of the truth manage to filter through, and by assembling all these fragments together, it is possible to begin to construct a more accurate representation of the socio-political conditions within the United States today.

It is notable that the typical reaction when information of this sort does appear in print is to deride it as yet further proof of the supposed "liberal" bias of the press. The notion that the American media has a liberal bias has never been remotely grounded in reality, but has rather been kept alive as a myth precisely so that embarrassing press coverage could be more easily discredited. As no less a conservative than Pat Buchanan has stated with uncharacteristic candor: "For heaven sakes, we kid about the liberal media, but every Republican on Earth does that."[1]

Another area of concern on the subject of sources is that of context. It will inevitably be charged that all of the excerpts and quotations contained in this book have been taken out of context. In a literal sense, this is of course quite true. Quoting material from another source requires, by definition, removing it from its original context. To do otherwise would require reproducing all of the source materials used in this book in their entirety.

This being an obviously unworkable proposition, the real question to be asked is: has this material been excerpted in such a way as to not fundamentally change its meaning in the original context in which it appeared. I think that I can, in good conscience, state that this is indeed the case here. Of course, every writer brings his own personal bias to his work, and it is entirely possible that this writer's bias has affected this work. To claim otherwise would reek of hypocrisy.

What do all these facts, taken together as a whole, add up to? The answer, which I believe will become increasingly apparent to the reader, is an ominous trend towards a more controlled, more authoritarian form of rule in the United States, leaving increasingly more democratic rights and freedoms lying in the wake of the reactionary agenda being sold to the American people.

It is precisely this trend, in all its various manifestations, that constitutes the hidden agenda being concealed by the American media. And it is also this trend that provides the common thread woven through each of the issues discussed in this book. Although the divisions are somewhat arbitrary, these issues are presented in seven sections, corresponding to the following general categories:

- Foreign relations
- The administration of justice
- Race issues
- The international arms trade
- The emerging police state
- The U.S. prison system
- Military issues and policy

In section one, we see America in the role of international outlaw, increasingly at odds with world opinion, as reflected in the United States' voting record on United Nations resolutions, as well as in a reluctance to ratify an array of international human rights treaties. Also featured here are a look at America's closed door policy on accepting political refugees and at the domestic and international implications of "globalization" and the concentration of wealth.

Sections two and three deal with racism and the administration of justice, two issues which regrettably often seem to overlap. What is portrayed is a nation still struggling with a firmly entrenched racism, as well as a criminal justice system wildly out of control, fueled by cynical politicians and a compliant media all too willing to sell unwarranted fear to the American people. The results are shown to include a rapidly increasing reliance on the use of the death penalty and a steady erosion of the barrier between youth and adult criminal justice.

The next section reveals that the United States has become the key player in the international arms trade, ahead of all other competitors combined. Along with this dubious distinction, America is seen to play a key role in the lesser known, though quite lucrative, markets in high tech surveillance equipment and torture devices—in other words, all the tools an oppressive foreign regime needs to maintain power against the will of its people.

Back on the domestic front, section five focuses on the various manifestations of what has been termed the prison-industrial complex. These include: skyrocketing incarceration rates, often in inhumane and brutal conditions; the proliferation of so-called "supermax" prisons; the trend towards the privatization of the prison industry; and the increasing use of prison labor by private sector corporations. The image created is of a self-perpetuating industry reliant on a steadily-increasing flow of inmates to maximize profits, dotting the landscape with prisons in the process.

Section six of the book looks at how modern surveillance technology has already made serious inroads into our privacy, revealing that George Orwell's 1984 might have arrived right on time after all—most of us just haven't been informed yet. Also in this section are chapters that detail other indications of a creeping police state mentality, including the role played by a seemingly harmless federal agency known as FEMA. The picture here is not a pretty one, as the walls of the prison state slowly expand to become the virtual walls of the police state.

The final section reveals a country increasingly reliant on military force as an agent of international diplomacy, developing new and alarming weapons systems to increase its already considerable military prowess. Also examined is the rarely reported human cost of our military exploits, with particular attention paid to Iraq. In sum, what is presented is a portrait of an America intent on becoming, or remaining, an international tyrant.

The final portion of the book, the epilogue, attempts to analyze these anti-democratic trends against the backdrop of the recent military actions in Kosovo, to provide a glimpse of how a more controlled, authoritarian and stratified America might look in the not too distant future. It is hoped that though this book is but one small voice of dissent straining to be heard over a well-orchestrated media barrage to the contrary, it will somehow be heard.

Greg Bates, my ever-vigilant editor at Common Courage Press, noted that the cover of this book presents something of a paradox—the photographic image used as the cover art, having originally appeared on the front page of the *Los Angeles Times*, the *New York Times*, and elsewhere, appears by its ubiquity to contradict this book's subtitle "The America the Media Don't Want You to See." But what do you see? While it is true that many will see in this image a graphic depiction of a police state response to peaceful, non-violent protestors exercising their constitutional right to air legitimate grievances, many others will see the justified response of a beleaguered and vastly outnumbered police force showing commendable restraint in using non-lethal means to control an unruly and violent mob. The interpretation one chooses is based on both personal biases and on the context in which the image is presented. It is clear from a reading of the stories that accompanied this image that it was the latter interpretation that the venerable *L.A. Times* meant to convey.

On December 7, 1999, this writer attended a FAIR (Fairness and Accuracy in Reporting) meeting in Santa Monica, California at which a version of the events in Seattle was presented that was considerably at odds with the portrayal by the media. A series of speakers, including California state senator Tom Hayden, gave first-person accounts of the appalling levels of violence employed by the Seattle police. Participants in the protests spoke of being repeatedly sprayed with tear gas and pepper spray, of being shot at point blank range with rubber bullets and bean bags, of demonstrators having their faces smashed into concrete, and of brutal assaults with police batons. They further pointed out that the demonstrations were overwhelmingly non-violent and orderly, with only a tiny fraction of the participants resorting to violent acts, and then only after unprovoked attacks by the riot-equipped officers. Of the nearly 600 arrested, only nine were charged with felony acts. All were for crimes against property; there were no arrests for acts of violence against another person.

This is strikingly at odds with the coverage afforded by the *L.A. Times* on December 1st and 2nd, as these events unfolded, which spoke of "a trashed downtown," of "police who battled rampaging protestors," and of "wide-spread vandalism and looting that swept through the city." Seattle police chief Norm Stamper was quoted commending his department for showing "remarkable restraint," and condemning the demonstrators for "the terror that was created in the hearts and minds of many people that were downtown." Mayor Paul Schell added that it was "painful for our officers to *stand there* and see people vandalizing their city (emphasis added)." By December 8, the slant of the coverage had become even more pronounced, as the *L.A. Times* reported that "outnumbered officers watched helplessly as mobs of World Trade Organization protestors rampaged through downtown Seattle—leaving behind $19 million in damages and lost retail sales," a grossly inflated figure based almost entirely on unsubstantiated estimates by retailers of lost sales.

This same front page story also carried a remarkable quote by Ken Saucier, an instructor at the Seattle police academy, which went unchallenged by the *L.A. Times*. Referring not to the treatment afforded the protestors, but of the conditions allegedly faced by his officers during the demonstrations, Mr. Saucier states, "Go to Amnesty International and ask them what the parameters for torture are. Those fit in those parameters."

Viewed in the context of these media reports, the picture on the cover of this book represented not revelations of heavy-handed police tactics (which my use of it is intended to suggest) but rather an image of valor and restraint. What you see will depend on the facts you bring to the picture. It is my hope that, whatever your starting perception, it will be different by the time you have finished reading this book.

David McGowan
January 2000

"You know the one thing that is wrong with this country? Everyone gets a chance to have their fair say."

President Clinton

"The Central Intelligence Agency owns everyone of any significance in the major media."

Former CIA Director William Colby

Section I

And Like a Good Neighbor...

CHAPTER 1

The Outlaw Nation

*Ironically, in light of its long-stated commitment to
upholding human rights at home and in its foreign policy, the
U.S. government today poses a threat to the universality
of human rights.*

— **Human Rights Watch "World
Report 1999, Introduction"**

*It is a paradox that the nation that did so much to articulate
and codify human rights in its foundation documents has so
consistently resisted the effective functioning of an international framework to protect these principles and values.*

— **Amnesty International "United States of America—
Rights for All," October 1998**

I n this chapter and the next, the focus will be on America's historical role in supporting the universal extension of human and
civil rights. Is the United States the number one defender of
human rights in the world today, as most Americans have been
taught by the schools and the media to believe? Or have the people
merely been fooled by the world's largest and most efficient propaganda machine? America's appalling record of ratifying human rights
treaties and its all-too-obvious contempt for international law and
world opinion reveals a far different face of America than that which
is presented to its citizens and to the world community at large.

WE'RE NUMBER ONE!

"No other democratic country in the world denies as many people—in absolute or proportional terms—the right to vote because of felony convictions."

Human Rights Watch "World Report 1999, United States"

AT LEAST WE'RE NOT THE ONLY ONES

"Every country on earth has ratified the United Nations' Convention on the Rights of the Child, which prohibits the death penalty for juvenile offenders, with two exceptions: Somalia, which effectively has no government, and the U.S. Even China, one of the world's most enthusiastic criminal-killers, recently banned juvenile executions."

"Wasted Youth," *The Mojo Wire,* **December 23, 1999**

"U.S. contempt for UN authority is shown by its defiance of the recent General Assembly vote of 157 nations versus 2 nations protesting the U.S. criminal blockade of Cuba..."

**Ramsey Clark (former U.S. Attorney General),
Letter to the UN, November 1998**

"The U.S.A. subsequently used its power of veto to prevent the UN Security Council taking action to implement the International Court's 1986 ruling on the Nicaraguan case. (Iran is the only other state not to have respected an International Court ruling.)"

**Amnesty International "United States of America—Rights
for All," October 1998, referring to the U.S. response
to the International Court's decision on the illegal
mining of Nicaragua's harbors.**

"The United Nations Commission on Human Rights, meeting in Geneva in April, called for a moratorium on all executions. The resolution was co-sponsored by 63 nations. The U.S. was one of the few countries to oppose it, along with such countries as Bangladesh, China, South Korea and Rwanda."

Death Penalty Information Center "The Death Penalty in 1998: Year End Report," December 1998

"And the United States was one of only seven states voting against the statute creating the ICC [International Criminal Court] at the Rome Diplomatic Conference in July; 120 states voted for the treaty."

Human Rights Watch "World Report 1999, United States," explaining how the U.S. opposed the creation of the legal entity which it then cynically proceeded to use to promote the war effort in Kosovo.

WE'RE GOING TO GET TO THAT, WE'VE JUST BEEN A LITTLE BUSY

"(T)he U.S.A. is also one of only a handful of countries that have not ratified the Convention on the Elimination of All Forms of Discrimination against Women."

Amnesty International "United States of America— Rights for All," October 1998

"The first UN human rights treaty ratified by the U.S.A. was the Convention on the Prevention and Punishment of the Crime of Genocide. It ratified the Convention in 1988, 40 years after signing it and after 97 other states had already ratified it. The U.S.A. took 28 years to ratify the International Convention on the Elimination of All Forms of Racial Discrimination, after 133 other states had already ratified it. At least 71 other states ratified the Convention against Torture before the U.S.A. It was only in 1992, after 109 other states, that the U.S.A. ratified the International Covenant on Civil and Political Rights (ICCPR), 26 years after its adoption by the UN General Assembly. The ICCPR is one of two principal treaties protecting human rights as enshrined in the Universal Declaration of Human Rights. The other—the International

Covenant on Economic, Social and Cultural Rights—has still not been ratified by the U.S.A…"

Amnesty International "United States of America—
Rights for All," October 1998

"(T)he U.S.A. has refused to recognize any regional human rights treaties: it has not ratified the American Convention on Human Rights, adopted by the OAS (Organization of American States) in 1969, and has not even signed the Inter-American Convention to Prevent and Punish Torture, the Inter-American Convention on Forced Disappearance of Persons and the Inter-American Convention to Prevent, Punish and Eradicate Violence against Women."

Amnesty International "United States of America—
Rights for All," October 1998

JUST PUT THAT ON MY TAB;
I'M GOOD FOR IT

"The United States has failed to pay its dues on time for the past 13 years…The UN says the United States is $1.69 billion in arrears; the U.S. government disputes the figure, maintaining that it owes about $1 billion."

The *Los Angeles Times*, June 24, 1999

WE'LL MAKE THE RULES
AND YOU FOLLOW THEM

"[T]o the detriment of the court [the ICC], its ability to acquire jurisdiction over a crime was significantly restricted in a futile effort to placate Washington…What Washington evidently wanted, and what the Rome delegates refused to cede, was the opportunity to exempt U.S. nationals altogether from the court's reach."

Human Rights Watch "World Report 1999, Introduction"

"In ratifying international human rights treaties it has typically carved away added protections for those in the United States by

18

adding reservations, declarations, and understandings. Even years after ratifying key human rights treaties, the U.S. still fails to acknowledge human rights law as U.S. law."

Human Rights Watch "World Report 1999, United States"

"[The U.S.] also is consistently late and superficial in reporting on its compliance with these treaties."

Human Rights Watch "World Report 1999, Introduction"

"One of the clearest examples of the U.S.A.'s changing attitude to human rights violations in different circumstances is that of Iraq. During the 1980s Iraqi forces committed gross and widespread abuses...Amnesty International repeatedly appealed for action, yet neither the U.S. authorities nor the UN responded...after Iraq invaded Kuwait in August 1990...The U.S.A. repeatedly cited the Iraqi government's appalling human rights record to gather support for UN military intervention in the Gulf."

**Amnesty International "United States of America—
Rights for All," October 1998**

MOVE ALONG FOLKS,
THERE'S NOTHING TO SEE HERE

"The U.S.A. has avoided scrutiny by international human rights protection bodies for many years...Human rights experts appointed by the UN Commission on Human Rights to investigate particular types of human rights abuse have not received full cooperation from the U.S. authorities. One such expert, the UN Special Rapporteur on extrajudicial, summary or arbitrary executions, was able to visit the U.S.A. only in late 1997, having repeatedly sought access since 1994."

**Amnesty International "United States of America—
Rights for All," October 1998**

WE DON'T LIKE TO LIMIT OUR OPTIONS

"[The U.S.] blocked international efforts to end the use of child soldiers, arguing against a proposed optional protocol to the Convention on the Rights of the Child that would raise the minimum age for military recruitment and participation in armed conflict to eighteen."

Human Rights Watch "World Report 1999, United States"

"In the case of landmines, the United States refused to join the 133 nations, including nearly every major U.S. ally, that had already signed the treaty by October 1998."

Human Rights Watch "World Report 1999, United States"

(In a seemingly deliberate and arrogant act of defiance of the global ban—set to go into effect on March 1, 1999—President Clinton, in February 1999, asked Congress to approve expenditures of nearly $50,000,000 to begin production of a new state-of-the-art artillery-fired landmine system.)

CHAPTER 2

Leading the Free World...But No One Is Following

There remains an organizing principle to the way the world works: if anything is going to get done, the U.S. is going to have to do it. The U.S. is, as Secretary of State Madeleine Albright likes to say, "the indispensable nation."

— **The *Wall Street Journal*, May 21, 1998**

That the United States is the leader of the free world is a truism known and accepted by virtually all Americans. Unfortunately, there is one minor problem with this self-evident "fact." In order for one to be a true leader, it is necessary for one to have followers. As the information in this chapter will illustrate, while the U.S. has certainly charted a rather unique and independent course, the rest of the world has notably failed to follow the leader. Listed below is a portion of the U.S. voting record in the UN on human rights issues affecting both specific groups and the world community as a whole. Though taken from a specific time period, namely the dawn of Reaganism, the voting pattern evident here does not markedly differ from that of other recent administrations. Each listing contains the resolution number, the date the measure was voted on, and the vote tally for and against. All dissenting votes were cast by the "leader of the free world," except as noted.

WHY IS EVERYONE LOOKING AT US?

Resolutions seeking to ban testing and development and prohibiting the proliferation of chemical and biological weapons:

36/96B	December 9, 1981	109-1
37/98A	December 13, 1982	95-1
38/187A	December 20, 1983	98-1
39/65B	December 12, 1984	84-1

Resolutions seeking to prohibit the testing and development of nuclear weapons:

37/73	December 9, 1982	111-1
37/78A	December 9, 1982	114-1
38/183M	December 20, 1983	133-1
39/148N	December 17, 1984	123-1

Resolutions seeking to prohibit the testing and development of *new* systems of "weapons of mass destruction":

38/182	December 20, 1983	116-1
39/62	December 12, 1984	125-1

Resolutions seeking to prohibit the escalation of the arms race into space:

37/83	December 9, 1982	138-1
38/70	December 15, 1983	147-1

JUST ME AND MY SHADOW

Resolutions in 1981 (a banner year) condemning Israel for various egregious human rights abuses committed against the

Palestinians. It is left to the reader to ponder which nation joined the United States to cast the second dissenting vote on each of these proposals.

36/15	October 28, 1981	114-2
36/73	December 4, 1981	109-2
36/120A	December 10, 1981	121-2
36/120E	December 10, 1981	139-2
36/146A	December 16, 1981	141-2
36/146C	December 16, 1981	117-2
36/146G	December 16, 1981	119-2
36/147C	December 16, 1981	111-2
36/147F	December 16, 1981	114-2
36/173	December 17, 1981	115-2
36/226B	December 17, 1981	121-2

WE VOTED OUR CONSCIENCE

Resolutions condemning various aspects of and/or calling for an end to apartheid in South Africa:

36/12	October 28, 1981	145-1
36/13	October 28, 1981	124-1
36/172C	December 17, 1981	136-1
36/172N	December 17, 1981	139-1
36/172O	December 17, 1981	138-1
37/47	December 3, 1982	124-1
37/69E	December 9, 1982	141-1
37/69G	December 9, 1982	138-1
37/69H	December 9, 1982	134-1
38/19	November 22, 1983	110-1
38/39E	December 5, 1983	149-1

| 38/39I | December 5, 1983 | 140-1 |
| 38/39K | December 5, 1983 | 145-1 |

THAT MIGHT CUT INTO PROFITS

Resolutions calling for education, health care, nourishment and national development to be considered basic human rights:

36/133	December 14, 1981	135-1
37/199	December 18, 1982	131-1
38/124	December 16, 1983	132-1

Protections against products that harm the environment and/or pose public health risks:

| 33/137 | December 17, 1982 | 146-1 |
| 41/450 | December 8, 1986 | 146-1 |

THAT WILL DEFINITELY CUT INTO PROFITS

Resolutions affirming the right of every nation to self determination of its economic and social systems free of outside intervention:

| 36/19 | November 9, 1981 | 126-1 |
| 38/25 | November 22, 1983 | 131-1 |

Resolution calling for a convention on the rights of the child:

| 42/101 | December 7, 1987 | 150-0-1 |
| | (The U.S. was the only nation to abstain) | |

All the material in this chapter was adapted from "The U.S. versus the World at the United Nations" by William Blum, author of *Killing Hope*.

CHAPTER 3

An Appointment with the Executioner

Paraguayan citizen Ángel Francisco Breard was executed in 1998 despite an International Court of Justice order that his execution should be suspended. Under the Vienna Convention on Consular Relations, to which the U.S.A. is party, Ángel Francisco Breard had the right to assistance from Paraguayan consular officials—assistance which he had been denied.

— Amnesty International "United States of America— Rights for All," October 1998

his case is featured here as a prime example of America's contempt for international law and world opinion. This case was notable in that it was the first time the World Court had ruled on a U.S. criminal case, and was also the first unanimous decision (15-0) ever issued against the United States. In addition, the countries of Mexico, Brazil, Ecuador, Paraguay and Argentina, together representing the majority of the world's Spanish speaking people, all filed briefs with the court opposing the execution, though to no avail. Breard's case serves as a portrait of America as the outlaw nation, holding itself above the law.

OUR LAWS ARE BETTER THAN YOUR LAWS

"Paraguay took his case to the International Court on the grounds that the Vienna Convention on Consular Relations had been violated. On 9 April 1998, the International Court ordered the execution to be suspended until it had considered the case—a decision that was binding on the U.S.A. under international law. Five days later, in flagrant defiance of the International Court's decision, the state authorities in Virginia executed Ángel Francisco Breard."

**Amnesty International "United States of America—
Rights for All," October 1998**

"For the first time, the International Court of Justice at The Hague asked that an execution in the U.S. be delayed, because a Paraguayan defendant's rights under the Vienna Convention had been violated. The World Court's request, along with a plea from Secretary of State Madeleine Albright, was rejected by the U.S. Supreme Court…and Ángel Breard was executed on April 14."

**Death Penalty Information Center "The Death Penalty
in 1998: Year End Report," December 1998**

I'M SURE IT WAS JUST AN ISOLATED CASE

"Four foreign nationals were also executed this year, three of whom challenged that they were not informed of their rights under the Vienna Convention to consult with their consulate at the time of their arrest."

**Death Penalty Information Center "The Death Penalty
in 1998: Year End Report," December 1998**

On March 3, 1999, German national Walter LaGrand was put to death by the state of Arizona despite protests from, and legal action by, the German government and the World Court. Like many others, Mr. LaGrand was denied consular access. This execution was notable for another reason as well—LaGrand became the only condemned prisoner this year to die in the gas chamber. The German people, with a unique historical perspective on the use of gas for executions, were understandably outraged. In September of 1999,

Germany announced that it intended to sue the United States in the International Court of Justice for violations of international law.

"It is barbaric and unworthy of a state based on the rule of law. It is appalling the way the death penalty is celebrated in Arizona. Apparently it's used for the re-election of governors and state prosecutors."

Herta Daeubler-Gmelin, German Justice Minister

"There is no doubt that international laws were violated. If the United States, the world's leading defender of democracy, doesn't respect international law, why should other countries?"

Claudia Roth, chairman of the German
Parliament's human rights committee

I'M THE LAW AROUND HERE

"(T)here's only one court that matters here. That's the U.S. Supreme Court. There's only one law that applies. That's the U.S. Constitution."

A spokesperson for Senate Foreign Relations Committee
Chairman Sen. Jesse Helms (R-NC), 1998

CHAPTER 4

The Insanity of Asylum Seekers

*Everyone has the right to seek and to enjoy asylum if they
are forced to flee their country to escape persecution. The
U.S.A. accepts this principle, and has agreed to be bound by
international standards to protect refugees. Yet U.S. authorities frequently violate the fundamental human rights of asylum-seekers by detaining them simply for seeking asylum...
U.S. policies and practices, which result in the indefinite
detention of most of those who seek asylum in the U.S.A.,
violate international human rights standards.*

**— Amnesty International "United States of America—
Rights for All," October 1998**

In keeping with America's decidedly anti-democratic stance on
international human rights issues, this chapter focuses on the
increasingly antagonistic position taken by the United States
towards those seeking political asylum from potentially life-threatening situations. America's door is effectively closed to those seeking
refuge. Equally troubling is that the U.S. has also pressured an array
of other allegedly democratic nations into likewise denying the right
of political asylum to those seeking it. The question that is never
raised is why the leader of the free world would adopt a policy so fundamentally at odds with the most basic precepts of human rights.

WELCOME TO AMERICA!
NOW GO HOME

"A new immigration act has led to a further sharp rise in detentions. In 1996 Congress enacted the Illegal Immigration Reform and Immigrant Responsibility Act (IIRIRA) which contains 'expedited removal provisions.' These allow the summary return of people seeking to enter the U.S.A…"

**Amnesty International "United States of America—
Rights for All," October 1998**

"Dennis McNamara, director of the UN Division of International Protection, said *Washington's practices have become so restrictive that they are now regularly cited by other governments as precedent in turning away people escaping life-threatening oppression and ethnic violence*…McNamara said he is urging the Clinton administration to reverse three policies he considers 'on a par' with the world's most restrictive rules: administrative detention of asylum-seekers; summary deportation; and expulsion of refugees convicted of felonies, even crimes such as passing bad checks."

The *Los Angeles Times*, March 6, 1999 (emphasis added)

WELCOME TO AMERICA!
NOW GO TO JAIL

"The number of those detained under the authority of the Immigration and Naturalization Services (INS) has soared, rising by 75 per cent between 1996 and 1998."

**Amnesty International "United States of America—
Rights for All," October 1998**

"INS detainees—including asylum seekers—were being held in jails entirely inappropriate to their non-criminal status, where they were often mixed with accused and convicted criminal inmates and where they were sometimes subjected to physical mistreatment and inadequate conditions of confinement."

Human Rights Watch "World Report 1999, United States"

XENOPHOBIA IS A RELATIVE CONCEPT

"Asylum-seekers are frequently denied access to visitors, to lawyers, to interpreters, to representatives from NGOs and other care-givers. Some face obstacles in making telephone calls and receiving letters or information essential for them to support their asylum claim…Asylum-seekers are shunted from one facility to another, across state lines, without any explanation other than that their bed space was needed. Little or no effort is made to keep asylum-seekers close to their families or sources of legal representation or to notify them that the asylum-seeker has been moved…In some cases the INS holds people in detention even though they have been granted asylum by immigration judges, while it appeals against the decision."

Amnesty International "United States of America—
Rights for All," October 1998

WHEN WE'RE DAMN GOOD AND READY

"Asylum-seekers in detention, unlike other prisoners, have no idea when they will be released."

Amnesty International "United States of America—
Rights for All," October 1998

WOMEN AND CHILDREN FIRST

"Women asylum-seekers are more likely to be detained together with criminal offenders than men. Their access to legal and social assistance is limited or non-existent…Children who need protection from persecution in their country of origin reportedly continue to be separated from their families and held in prison-like conditions, in breach of international standards."

Amnesty International "United States of America—
Rights for All," October 1998

"Some unaccompanied minors were housed with juvenile offenders, locked up and made to wear prison uniforms even though they were held for administrative reasons only."

Human Rights Watch "World Report 1999, United States"

AND DON'T THINK ANYONE ELSE IS GOING TO HELP EITHER

"The United States worked for four months to help Turkey arrest Abdullah Ocalan, the Kurdish rebel leader, U.S. officials said on Friday. U.S. diplomatic pressure backed by intelligence gathering helped to put Ocalan in flight from a safe haven in Syria, to persuade nation after nation to refuse him sanctuary and to drive him into an increasingly desperate search for a city of refuge, the officials said... From October onward, as Ocalan sought shelter in Russia, across Europe and in Africa, U.S. diplomats and intelligence officers sought to cut off his escape routes...They placed the Greek Embassy under surveillance and monitored Ocalan's cell phone conversations, while he placed calls to political contacts, seeking sanctuary...They warned their European and Russian counterparts of the consequences of sheltering Ocalan..."

The *New York Times*, February 1999

I'M SURE HE'LL BE TREATED FAIRLY BY OUR NATO PARTNER

"(T)orture in detention remained widespread. In late 1997, when Minister of Foreign Affairs Ismail Cem referred to torture as an agonizing disgrace in the country, he became the highest state official to date to have acknowledged the extent of the problem...A court acquitted ten policemen accused of torturing fourteen teenagers from the town of Manisa, despite the fact that Sabri Ergul, a lawyer and member of parliament, testified that he had witnessed the torture, and hospital records supported the charges of police brutality. The Manisa teenagers, eight of whom were under eighteen when they were detained, testified that they had been beaten, raped with truncheons, and given electric shocks...In April, when six police officers were sentenced to five and a half years each for torturing a suspect to death in 1993, the defendants and about sixty plainclothes policemen brutally beat the victim's sister and lawyer in the courtroom. The policemen appealed the verdict...Extra-judicial killings by police forces during house raids or demonstrations had become common in Turkey after the Anti-Terror Law entered into force in 1991...The investigating parliamentarians described as 'atrocious' the conditions at the Juvenile Prison, where an undercover journalist from the mainstream media had witnessed during regular visiting hours seven or eight guards beating a child."

Human Rights Watch "World Report 1999, Turkey"

JUSTICE, AMERICAN STYLE

"Despite vigorous debates [in Turkey] among state officials and in civil society on the 'rule of law,' laws continued to be applied arbitrarily..."

Human Rights Watch "World Report 1999, Turkey"

CHAPTER 5

For Richer...
For Poorer

I see in the near future a crisis approaching that unnerves me and causes me to tremble for the safety of my country...corpora-tions have been enthroned and an era of corruption in high places will follow, and the money of the country will endeavor to pro-long its reign by working upon the prejudices of the people until all wealth is aggregated in a few hands and the Republic is destroyed. I feel at this moment more anxiety for the safety of my country than ever before, even in the midst of war.

— President Abraham Lincoln

[W]e have about 50% of the world's wealth, but only 6.3% of its population...In this situation, we cannot fail to be the object of envy and resentment. Our real task in the coming period is to devise a pattern of relationships which will permit us to maintain this position of disparity.

**— U.S. State Department Policy
Planning Study #23, 1948**

Global inequalities in income and living standards have reached grotesque proportions.

**— United Nations Development Program
"Human Development Report, 1999"**

Paralleling the trend towards a more authoritarian form of rule is a trend towards an increasingly stratified society, with an inordinate amount of the nation's and the world's wealth consolidated into the hands of the few. This is not an unrelated occurrence, but is rather the primary reason for the shift away from democratic rule. When income disparity reaches extreme levels, no amount of propaganda can legitimize the system, and increased levels of force become necessary. In late June of 1999, *Forbes* magazine released its annual list of the 200 wealthiest individuals in the world. By far the most striking feature of the list is the degree to which the world's wealth is being concentrated in the hands of American multi-billionaires. Presented below are the lists of the top ten richest people worldwide for the years 1996–1999, courtesy of *Forbes*, showing a rather remarkable pattern:

1996

1.	**Gates, William**	**United States**	**$18.5 billion**
2.	**Buffet, Warren**	**United States**	**$15 billion**
3.	Oeri, Hoffman and Sacher families	Switzerland	$13.1 billion
4.	Lee Shau Kee	Hong Kong	$12.7 billion
5.	Tsai Wan-lin Family	Taiwan	$12.2 billion
6.	Kwok Brothers	Hong Kong	$11.2 billion
7.	Li Ka-shing Family	Hong Kong	$10.6 billion
8.	Tsutsumi, Yoshiaki	Japan	$9.2 billion
9.	Albrecht, Theo and Karl	Germany	$9 billion
10.	Rausing, Hans and Gad	Scandinavia	$9 billion

Number of Americans in top ten: **2**

Top ten assets held by Americans: **$33.5 billion**

Percentage of total top ten wealth held by Americans: **28%**

<u>1997</u>

1.	Bolkiah, Sultan Hassanal	Brunei	$38 billion
2.	**Gates, William**	**United States**	**$36.4 billion**
3.	**Walton Family**	**United States**	**$27.6 billion**
4.	**Buffett, Warren**	**United States**	**$23.2 billion**
5.	Alsaud, King Faud Bin Abdul Aziz	Saudi Arabia	$20 billion
6.	Suharto	Indonesia	$16 billion
7.	**Allen, Paul Gardner**	**United States**	**$15.3 billion**
8.	Al-Sabah, Sheikh Jaber Al-ahmed Al-jaber	Kuwait	$15 billion
9.	Lee Shau Kee	Hong Kong	$14.7 billion
10.	Oeri, Hoffman and Sacher families	Switzerland	$14.3 billion

Number of Americans in top ten: **4**
Top ten assets held by Americans: **$102.5 billion**
Percentage of total top ten wealth held by Americans: **46%**

<u>1998</u>

1.	**Gates, William**	**United States**	**$51billion**
2.	**Walton Family**	**United States**	**$48 billion**
3.	Bolkiah, Sultan Hassanal	Brunei	$36 billion
4.	**Buffett, Warren**	**United States**	**$33 billion**
5.	Alsaud, King Faud Bin Abdul Aziz	Saudi Arabia	$25 billion
6.	**Allen, Paul Gardner**	**United States**	**$21 billion**
7.	Al Nahyan, Sheikh Zayed Bin Sultan	UAE	$15 billion
8.	Al-Sabah, Sheikh Jaber Al-ahmed Al-jaber	Kuwait	$15 billion

| 9. | Thomson, Kenneth | Canada | $14.4 billion |
| 10. | Pritzker, Jay A. and Robert A. | United States | $13.5 billion |

Number of Americans in top ten: 5
Top ten assets held by Americans: *$166.5 billion*
Percentage of top ten wealth held by Americans: 61%

<u>1999</u>

1.	Gates, William	United States	$90 billion
2.	Buffett, Warren	United States	$36 billion
3.	Allen, Paul Gardner	United States	$30 billion
4.	Ballmer, Steven	United States	$19.5 billion
5.	Anschutz, Philip	United States	$16.5 billion
6.	Dell, Michael	United States	$16.5 billion
7.	Walton, S. Robson	United States	$15.8 billion
8.	Alsaud, Prince Alwaleed Bin Talal	Saudi Arabia	$15 billion
9.	Albrecht, Theo & Karl	Germany	$13.6 billion
10.	Li Ka-shing and family	Hong Kong	$12.6 billion

Number of Americans in top ten: 7
Top ten assets held by Americans: *$224.3 billion*
Percentage of top ten wealth held by Americans: 84%

OBSERVATIONS ON THE CONCENTRATION OF WEALTH...

- This pattern extends beyond the top ten. Among the 25 wealthiest individuals in the world, 12 are now Americans with combined assets of 273.3 billion dollars. Three years ago, there were just five Americans in this group with combined assets of only 54.2 billion dollars.

- Whenever attending an all-you-can-eat buffet, always try to position yourself in line well ahead of any American billionaires in the crowd.

ON GLOBALIZATION...

Premise 1: Wealth is created by the combined labor and effort of hundreds of millions of workers around the world. Once created, wealth does not simply vanish.

Premise 2: Wall Street does not create or destroy wealth. The stock and bond markets serve only to transfer and redistribute wealth, creating nothing.

Premise 3: American productivity has not drastically increased in recent years, thereby creating vast stockpiles of new wealth in this country.

- In the last few years, many countries have been economically devastated by currency devaluation caused by external manipulations of their markets. In places such as Mexico and Indonesia, vast portions of the nation's wealth seemed to vanish virtually overnight.

- In a completely unrelated economic development, American billionaires have accumulated almost incomprehensible personal fortunes in recent years.

- It's a good thing these two trends are unrelated or some people might start to think that America was systematically siphoning off the world's wealth.

- In other completely unrelated news, the International Federation of Red Cross and Red Crescent Societies released a report recently (World Disasters Report 1999) that predicts a "decade of super-disasters." It seems that "the explosive combination of human-driven climate change and rapidly changing socio-economic conditions will set off chain reactions of devastation...Everyone is aware of the environmental problems of global warming and deforestation on the one hand, and the social problems of increasing poverty and growing shanty towns on the other. But when these two factors collide, you have a new scale of catastrophe."

- In a similar vein, the UN Environmental Program (UNEP) end-of-century review, "Global Environment Outlook 2000," warns of a variety of "full scale emergencies" looming on the horizon, and concludes that the "continued poverty of the majority of the planet's inhabitants and excessive consumption by the minority are the two major causes of environmental degradation."

- To clarify the above, the influx of wealth into the United States has nothing to do with increased poverty and the proliferation of shanty towns elsewhere, and U.S. business practices have done nothing to contribute to so-called global warming and deforestation, which are in reality just fabrications of the liberal media, even if NASA did acknowledge that "Global surface temperatures in 1998 set a new record by a wide margin,"[2] and even if "(P)resident (Clinton) had to acknowledge that his country was the main offender, producing more greenhouse gases than any other country in the world,"[3] and even if the UNEP did report that "the destruction of tropical rainforests has already gone too far to prevent irreversible damage and it is too late to regain the planet's former bio-diversity."[4]

FURTHER OBSERVATIONS
ON GLOBALIZATION...

Another recently released report comes from the United Nations Development Program, entitled "Human Development Report 1999" (UNHDR). This report reveals some of the harsh realities of globalization and the attendant consolidation of wealth into the hands of the few, as these excerpts illustrate:

- "The income gap between the fifth of the world's people living in the richest countries and the fifth in the poorest was 74 to 1 in 1997, up from 60 to 1 in 1990 and 30 to 1 in 1960."

- "By the late 1990s the fifth of the world's people living in the highest income countries had...86% of the world GDP (Gross Domestic Product)—the bottom fifth just 1%."

- "To sum up: the top fifth of the world's people in the richest countries enjoy 82% of the expanding export trade and 68% of foreign direct investment—the bottom fifth, barely more than 1%."

- "The net worth of the world's 200 richest people increased from $440 billion to more than $1 trillion in just the four years from 1994 to 1998."

- "The assets of the three richest people were more than the combined GNP of the 48 least developed countries." (Comprising some *600 million people*.)

- "The assets of the 200 richest people are more than the combined income of 41% of the world's people."

The report also presents evidence that globalization is succeeding quite well at spreading some of the more salient features of modern American democracy. Discussing the financial crisis in East Asia in the late 1990s, for instance, it is duly noted that "Bankruptcies spread. Education and health budgets came under pressure. More than 13 million people lost their jobs," after which the full extent to which the global village has assumed an American flavor is then revealed:

- "The consequences go deeper—all countries report erosion of their social fabric, with social unrest, more crime, more violence in the home."

ON MICROSOFT AND MONOPOLY POWER...

In an *L.A. Times* editorial published June 25, 1999, just days before the release of the *Forbes* list, the paper opined that "The (Microsoft anti-trust) trial uncovered overwhelming evidence that Microsoft has behaved as the worst kind of bullying monopolist."

ıg as a "bullying monopolist," it should be noted, has
Gates a personal fortune of $90 billion, making him far
___ ıy the richest man in the world. Two of Microsoft's exec-
utives join him on the list as the third and fourth richest men in
the world.

- Behaving as a "bullying monopolist," it should also be noted, is
criminal behavior. Among other things, it is a form of theft, in
this case on a scale never before seen by humankind.

- Despite acknowledging that Microsoft's business practices are
illegal, the *Times* nevertheless recommends a "voluntary settle-
ment" as the best solution "for consumers" so as to avoid "hob-
bling one of the American economy's growth engines."

- In completely unrelated news, the same *L.A. Times* reported on
March 3, 1995 that "Jerry Dewayne Williams was sentenced to
prison for 25 years to life Thursday under the state's 'three
strikes' law for stealing a slice of pepperoni pizza."

- Interestingly, the UNHDR informs us that "Criminals are reap-
ing the benefits of globalization," though it fails to specify if
these are criminals of the pizza-stealing type or of the bullying-
monopolist type.

ON THE BOOMING U.S. ECONOMY....

Just after the release of the *Forbes* list, deep within the bowels of
the July 1st edition, the *Los Angeles Times* offered two articles that
gave further evidence of the booming economy that has enriched
America's billionaires. One of these articles reported that "Every
night, more than one million children in America face the dark
with no place to call home...Experts say that there are more home-
less children in America than at any time since the Great
Depression." The second article notes that a study by the Census
Bureau "found that 7.7% of American children—about 5.5 million—lived with a grandparent...the social consequences for these
children include a greater likelihood that they will be raised in
poverty."

- This would tend to indicate that not all of the wealth accumulated by American billionaires was siphoned off of foreign markets. Some of it was stolen right here at home, through the trickle-up economic model characterized by such features as "corporate welfare," negligible social spending, high-income tax cuts, and corporate downsizings.

- The combined assets of Captain Bill and his two lieutenants at Microsoft is a truly staggering $139.5 billion.

- Assuming the average selling price for a home nationwide is $100,000, and assuming the number of homeless kids in America is indeed one million, these three men alone could buy each of these kids their very own home.

- Further assuming that the three men were then to equally divide their remaining combined assets, each of them would retain enough personal wealth to remain among the ten wealthiest men in the world, although Bill would have to forfeit the number 1 spot to fellow American Warren Buffett.

- In news that would seem to be related but is not, the UNHDR reports that "A yearly contribution of 1% of the wealth of the 200 richest people could provide universal access to primary education for all."

FINAL NOTES ON BILL GATES...

- Bill Gates acquired so much wealth in the last year alone that had he begun the year with nothing, and his total net worth was limited to his 1999 earnings, he would still be the richest man in the world.

- In the time you spent reading this chapter, Bill Gates probably made more money than you will make in your entire life. Not that there's anything wrong with that.

"We can have democracy in this country, or we can have great wealth concentrated in the hands of a few, but we can't have both."

Louis Brandeis, United States Supreme Court
Justice from 1916–1939

"We stand for the maintenance of private property...We shall protect free enterprise as the most expedient, or rather the sole possible economic order."

Adolph Hitler

Section II

The Rule of Law

CHAPTER 6

To Protect and to Serve

There is a widespread and persistent problem of police brutality across the U.S.A. Thousands of individual complaints about police abuse are reported each year and local authorities pay out millions of dollars to victims in damages after lawsuits…in the past eight years independent inquiries have uncovered systematic abuses in some of the country's largest city police departments, revealing a serious nationwide problem.

— **Amnesty International "United States of America— Rights for All," October 1998**

The violations persisted nationwide, in rural, suburban, and urban areas of the country, committed by various law enforcement personnel including local and state police, sheriff's departments, and federal agents. Police have engaged in unjustified shootings, severe beatings, fatal chokings, and unnecessarily rough treatment.

— **Human Rights Watch "World Report 1999, United States"**

The problem of police abuse in America, in cities both large and small, is quite pervasive, though the issue only comes to widespread public attention in extreme cases such as the infamous videotaped Rodney King beating. In these cases, the "bad apple" theory is inevitably trotted out by the offending department to explain what is described as an atypical occurrence. Once the bad apples have been weeded out, we are assured, all will be well again. Unfortunately, this explanation willfully and deliberately masks the very firmly entrenched and often racially motivated nature of police brutality in this country. Due to reasons revealed in the first pair of excerpts presented here, no statistical evidence exists to document whether such brutality is indeed on the rise; what anecdotal evidence is available, however, indicates this could well be the case.

WE SPENT THE MONEY GIVING
OURSELVES ANOTHER PAY RAISE

"Since 1994, the federal government has been legally required [by the Violent Crime and Control Act] to collect national data on police use of excessive force, but congress has failed to provide the funding necessary for it to do so."

**Amnesty International "United States of America—
Rights for All," October 1998**

"[D]espite a four-year-old congressional mandate, the Justice Department still has not taken serious steps to document the scope of police brutality in the United States."

Human Rights Watch "World Report 1999, Introduction"

I LOVE L.A.

"Two official inquiries into policing in Los Angeles found a serious problem of excessive use of force, including beatings and unjustified shootings by patrol officers, perpetrated mainly against members of minority groups…There have been allegations of unwarranted shootings during police stakeouts. Particular concern has been raised about the activities of the LAPD's Special Investigation Squad (SIS), an elite surveillance squad. According to media reports, the City of Los Angeles has paid $1.9m in damages arising from SIS actions...Hog-tying was banned within the LAPD only in August 1997, despite dozens of deaths in LAPD custody since the mid-1980s of suspects who were hog-tied."

Amnesty International "United States of America— Rights for All," October 1998

NEVER LEAVE HOME WITHOUT YOUR CAMCORDER

"Weak civilian review, flawed internal investigations, and rare criminal prosecutions by federal or local prosecutors virtually guaranteed that officers who engaged in brutality would avoid punishment of any kind."

Human Rights Watch "World Report 1999, United States"

"Brutality following challenges to police authority (widely known as 'contempt of cop') has been widely documented"

Amnesty International "United States of America— Rights for All," October 1998

IT DEPENDS ON HOW YOU DEFINE "CRUEL AND UNUSUAL"

"Allegations of systematic torture in one police station over a 20-year period came to light in 1989, involving at least 65 suspects who reported torture including electric shocks and having plastic bags placed over their heads...There have been numerous deaths in police custody following restraint procedures known to be dangerous. Suspects have died after being placed face-down in restraints, usually while 'hog-tied' (where a suspect's ankles are bound from behind to the wrists), or after pressure has been applied to the neck or chest...Since the early 1990s, more than 60 people in the U.S.A.

are reported to have died in police custody after being exposed to OC (pepper) spray."

**Amnesty International "United States of America—
Rights for All," October 1998**

IN EL SALVADOR, THEY CALL
THOSE "DEATH SQUADS"

- February 5, 1999; New York City: Four police officers, working in plain clothes as part of an "elite" unit, shot 41 times at an unarmed man (Amadou Diallo) in front of his home, hitting him 19 times and killing him. Two of the officers emptied their 16 shot clips. One of the officers was already under investigation for a previous fatal shooting in October of 1997. Three of the four had used their guns previously, a rather remarkable fact given that most officers have never fired their weapons on duty. These three officers collectively had received at least 11 prior complaints of excessive force, abuse of authority and other related charges. The NYPD has not yet offered an explanation for the shooting.

- December 28, 1998; Riverside, California: Tyisha Miller, a 19-year-old black girl, was found locked in her car, asleep or unconscious in the driver's seat. A gun was reportedly in her lap. When the police revived her by breaking the driver's window, they claim she reached for the gun. The officers fired 24 shots, killing her instantly. The district attorney has declined to file any charges against the officers in the case.

- During the first weekend in June 1999, Chicago police shot and killed two unarmed people during traffic stops in separate incidents. It was reported that one of them, LaTanya Haggerty, "had her hands in the air and was telling officers she was getting out of a car when she was shot," according to an eyewitness. **The *Los Angeles Times*, June 13, 1999**

I THINK WE MIGHT HAVE HIT HIM

- March 27, 1998; Los Angeles: "Los Angeles County sheriff's deputies, Hawthorne police and California Highway Patrol officers had shot Michael William Arnold **106 times…at least 55 of the wounds were serious enough to be fatal**." Police claimed that Arnold brandished a weapon, later identified as an air gun, and that "when coroner's investigators arrived several hours after the shooting, they found Arnold clutching the air pistol in his right hand." The chief medical examiner noted, however, that for Arnold to still be clutching the gun "when he was down and dead, that is extremely unlikely, because he was shot in the right arm and also several shots went through the head." The victim's mother noted "the autopsy finding that her son had been shot three times in his right hand," miraculously without hitting the gun he was allegedly holding. Also notable is that investigators "lifted gunshot residue from Arnold's right hand." As a coroner's spokesman noted, "You can't get gunshot residue from firing an air gun," though "if someone who had fired a weapon touched his hands, you could transfer the residue." **The Los Angeles Times, July 26, 1999 (emphasis added)**

CHAPTER 7

The Rising Body Count

More than 100 countries have now abolished the death penalty in law or practice...Against the global trend towards abolition, however, the U.S.A. has relentlessly increased its rate of executions and the number of crimes punishable by death.

— Amnesty International "United States of America— Rights for All," October 1998

The use of the death penalty, considered a barbaric abuse of human rights throughout most of the world, has for some time now been sold to the American people as the antidote to rising levels of violent crime in society. Far from deterring crime, however, executions serve to foster yet more violence by legitimizing the use of deadly force. Increasingly, family and friends of the victim of the accused are encouraged to participate in the blood lust by attending the execution. There is even talk occasionally of televising these events for all to see. The net effect of these ghoulish exhibitions is to further desensitize the American people to the use of state violence, and thereby lower the resistance to even greater use of state oppressive force.

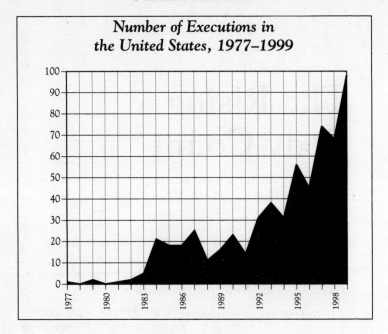

Number of Executions in the United States, 1977–1999

WE'RE NUMBER 1

"The U.S.A. has the highest known death row population on earth: over 3,300 people await their deaths at the hands of U.S. authorities."

Amnesty International "United States of America—Rights for All," October 1998

"The number of people on death row again moved to a record high and now stands at 3,517…"

Death Penalty Information Center "The Death Penalty in 1998: Year End Report," December 1998

AT LEAST WE'RE IN GOOD COMPANY

"In 1997 the U.S.A. carried out 74 executions—the highest number for four decades. Only China, Saudi Arabia and Iran were known to have executed more prisoners."

**Amnesty International "United States of America—
Rights for All," October 1998**

"[O]nly five other countries are known to have executed juvenile offenders in the 1990s: Pakistan, Saudi Arabia, Iran, Nigeria, and Yemen. The U.S. has executed more juvenile criminals than all of them combined—and is the only one known to have put any to death since 1997."

"Wasted Youth," *The Mojo Wire*, December 23, 1999

WELL, THEY SURE LOOKED GUILTY

"At least 75 wrongly convicted people have been released from death row since 1973."

**Amnesty International "United States of America—
Rights for All," October 1998**

"In 1989 the Supreme Court ruled that it was not unconstitutional for the death penalty to be used against mentally retarded defendants. Some 30 prisoners suffering from mental disabilities have been executed since this ruling."

**Amnesty International "United States of America—
Rights for All," October 1998**

"Tuan Nguyen was executed in Oklahoma on December 10, the 50th anniversary of the UN Universal Declaration of Human Rights... His attorneys reported a complete inability to communicate with him over the past nine years, despite numerous attempts... Despite claims that he was incompetent to be executed, the Supreme Court refused, by a vote of 5-4, to stay his execution."

**Death Penalty Information Center "The Death Penalty
in 1998: Year End Report," December 1998**

IF WE WAIT TOO LONG, SOME OF THEM MIGHT BE ABLE TO PROVE THEIR INNOCENCE

"In 1996, President Clinton signed the Anti-Terrorism and Effective Death Penalty Act into law. The Act, designed to reduce the time between sentence and execution, severely limits the appeals available to death row inmates in federal courts."

> **Amnesty International "United States of America—
> Rights for All," October 1998**

"In Mississippi, the state Supreme Court declared that indigent death row inmates are entitled to representation, but the legislature has not approved a single dollar to implement that ruling."

> **Death Penalty Information Center "The Death Penalty
> in 1998: Year End Report," December 1998**

YOU SNOOZE, YOU LOSE

"Thomas Thompson was executed in California on July 14. The U.S. Court of Appeals for the Ninth Circuit had stopped an earlier execution date and reversed his conviction because of ineffective assistance of counsel. The U.S. Supreme Court, however, overturned the appellate court's decision because, it said, the Ninth Circuit had acted too late."

> **Death Penalty Information Center "The Death Penalty
> in 1998: Year End Report," December 1998**

"Roger Coleman was represented at trial by lawyers who had never handled a murder case before. They failed to prepare adequately or to investigate evidence, including his alibi, and presented no mitigation. On appeal Roger Coleman was represented by volunteer lawyers unfamiliar with Virginia courts. They inadvertently filed the notice to appeal to the State Supreme Court one day late, and as a result the Court dismissed the appeal without a hearing. In 1991 the U.S. Supreme Court ruled that Roger Coleman had lost his right to federal review because of his lawyers' mistake. Roger

Coleman was executed in 1992 despite serious doubts about his guilt."

Amnesty International "United States of America—
Rights for All," October 1998

INNOCENCE IS NO EXCUSE FOR BREAKING THE LAW

"(T)he Supreme Court ruled that errors by lawyers would not merit the reversal of the conviction or sentence unless the defendant could prove that such errors had prejudiced the outcome of the case, a standard of proof that is very difficult to meet. The Court stated that: 'the government is not responsible for, and hence not able to prevent, attorney errors.' The result of this ruling has been that prisoners may have been executed as a result of mistakes by their lawyers."

Amnesty International "United States of America—
Rights for All," October 1998

"Leonel Herrera was executed in Texas after the U.S. Supreme Court denied his appeal despite newly discovered evidence that appeared to show he was innocent. The Court ruled that there was no constitutional right to federal intervention because of new evidence where the original trial had been free from procedural error. In a strongly worded dissent, three justices argued that the Constitution's protection against cruel and unusual punishments did not end once a defendant had been sentenced to death, and that '[t]he execution of a person who can show that he is innocent comes perilously close to simple murder.' "

Amnesty International "United States of America—
Rights for All," October 1998

THE COURT OF LAST RESORT

"In *McCleskey v. Kemp*, the U.S. Supreme Court held that the defendant had to show that he was personally discriminated against in the course of the prosecution. 'Merely' showing a disturbing pattern of racial disparities in Georgia over a long period of time was not sufficient to prove bias in his case."

Death Penalty Information Center (DPIC) "The Death Penalty in Black & White," June 1998

"(T)he Supreme Court concluded that 'apparent disparities in sentencing are an inevitable part of the criminal justice system' and that any system for determining guilt or punishment 'has its weaknesses and potential for misuse.' However, the Court ruled that the defendant, Warren McCleskey, had failed to prove that the decision-makers in his particular case had acted with discriminatory intent...Warren McCleskey was executed in 1991."

Amnesty International "United States of America—Rights for All," October 1998

"In refusing to grant a stay to review fully McCleskey's claims, the Court values expediency over human life. Repeatedly denying Warren McCleskey his constitutional rights is unacceptable. Executing him is inexcusable."

United States Supreme Court Justice Thurgood Marshall

"(The) risk that race influenced McCleskey's sentence is intolerable by any imaginable standard."

United States Supreme Court Justice William Brennan

"When in *Gregg v. Georgia* the Supreme Court gave its seal of approval to capital punishment, this endorsement was premised on the promise that capital punishment would be administered with fairness and justice. Instead, the promise has become a cruel and empty mockery. If not remedied, the scandalous state of our present system of capital punishment will cast a pall of shame over our society for years to come. We cannot let it continue."

United States Supreme Court Justice Thurgood Marshall, 1990

CHAPTER 8

The War on Childhood

Ironically, America's juvenile court, which was the first court in the world to recognize the need to separate juveniles from adults, was founded in 1899 when women did not yet have the right to vote, and segregation was still the law of the land. In our present state of media-driven hysteria, we are dangerously close to reverting to a 19th Century mode of jurisprudence. As we enter the new millennium, this would be a baneful legacy to bequeath to our next generation.

— **Vincent Schiraldi (Director, Justice Policy Intsitute) in the *Christian Science Monitor*, November 1997**

There has been a deliberate effort made in this country to condition the American people to accept ever-increasing levels of state-sanctioned violence against juveniles, including incarceration in adult facilities and even the executions of individuals for offenses committed as minors. Sensationalizing of crime—particularly recent schoolyard shootings and urban gang violence—by the mass media, and the cynical "tough on crime" stance taken by virtually all politicians of both major parties, have whetted the public's appetite for what were previously considered barbaric judicial measures. The scapegoating of youth, long a favorite pastime of the media and many politicians, has increased markedly in recent years. Hidden beneath all the cynical rhetoric, and obscured by the high profile given to isolated acts of extreme violence, is the fact that overall rates of youth crime have actually declined. Also obscured and unmentioned is the fact that our youth are among the most frequent, and the most vulnerable, *victims* of crime in this country, much of which goes unreported in the form of domestic violence, by far the most frequently committed crime in America.

JUST THINK OF IT AS A "BIG BROTHER" PROGRAM

"Recent state legislation has increased the number of children held in adult facilities and proposed legislation would further weaken existing protection for children...In at least 20 states, children who are convicted as adults may be sentenced to imprisonment in adult prisons and housed with adult inmates."

**Amnesty International "United States of America—
Rights for All," October 1998**

"Between 1992 and 1998, at least forty states adopted legislation making it easier for children to be tried as adults, and forty-two states detained juveniles in adult jails while they awaited trial."

Human Rights Watch "World Report 1999, United States"

EQUALITY UNDER THE LAW

"At the time of writing, congress was considering legislation designed to encourage the prosecution of children as adults under federal and state laws."

**Amnesty International "United States of America—
Rights for All," October 1998**

HAVEN'T I HEARD THOSE NAMES BEFORE?

"For the past two years, Congressman Bill McCollum (R-Florida) has authored radical legislation to overhaul America's juvenile justice system. His bill goes so far as to allow juveniles as young as age 13 to be jailed with adults, prior to even being convicted of any crimes."

Vincent Schiraldi in the *Christian Science Monitor*, November 1997 (Joining McCollum in sponsoring this bill were fellow impeachment zealots Henry Hyde, Ed Bryant, Steven Buyer, and Howard Coble)

KIDS IN THE NEWS

- Tallahassee, Florida: In February of 1998, Chaquita Doman was arrested and booked *as a felon* following a relatively minor schoolyard altercation. Chaquita was *five years old*.

- Pontiac, Michigan: Nathaniel Abraham, 12 years old, is being tried and will be sentenced as an adult. Nathaniel was only 11 at the time he allegedly committed an act of murder, which he claims was an accident. Psychiatrists who have examined him say that his mental functioning is at the level of a 6 year old. Nathaniel's "confession" to his interrogators, obtained without counsel present, was admitted into evidence by the judge, who apparently felt that a child understands the implications of waiving his constitutional rights.

- Oklahoma: On February 4, 1999, Sean Sellers was executed for crimes that he committed at the age of 16. In 1998, there were only 3 known judicial executions of juvenile offenders carried out in the entire world. All three were in the United States.

- Barstow, Florida: In August of 1999, Joshua Phillips was sentenced to life in prison with no possibility of parole. Joshua was 14 at the time of his arrest for murder. In reporting the story on August 21, the *L.A. Times* lamented that "Florida law bars the death penalty for killers younger than 16."

"Today, the Supreme Court has set 16 as the minimum age for death penalty eligibility, but there are many who would like to see that lowered. Former California Gov. Pete Wilson suggested lowering the age limit to 14, and a Texas state legislator has introduced a bill to make it 11."

"Wasted Youth," *The Mojo Wire*, **December 23, 1999**

CHAPTER 9

The Politics of Fear

Voice or no voice, the people can always be brought to the bidding of the leaders. That is easy. All you have to do is to tell them they are being attacked, and denounce the pacifists for lack of patriotism and exposing the country to danger.

— **Hermann Goering, at the Nuremberg Trials**

Our government has kept us in a perpetual state of fear—kept us in a continuous stampede of patriotic fervor—with the cry of grave national emergency. Always there has been some terrible evil at home or some monstrous foreign power that was going to gobble us up if we did not blindly rally behind it...

— **General Douglas McArthur, 1957**

The current appearance of solving the crime problem is nothing more than politicians heightening people's fears in order to assuage them. Crime rates have been essentially stable since the 1970s. Politicians use a "bait and switch" scam in which they treat rare and horrifying crimes as if they are typical— switching voter outrage at the horrible crime to punishment of lesser and non-violent offenders.

— **National Criminal Justice Commission, February 1996**

Selling fear to the American people has become a mainstay of the press and of both political parties in this country. Taking a "tough on crime" stance, particularly in a climate of perpetual fear created by the "war on drugs" and the "war on terrorism," is always a politically safe posture. "Criminals" have no lobbying groups; there is no political price to pay for attacking such an easy scapegoat, particularly one that has by and large forfeited the right to vote. By focusing on crime, attention is effectively directed away from more divisive issues on which a politician might have to take a stand that would cost them votes. Meanwhile, a fearful populace continues to surrender their civil rights and constitutional protections at an alarming rate, so that their government may protect them from the rampant criminality of the masses.

YOU MEAN THE SKY ISN'T FALLING?

"Between 1992 and 1993, major network evening news coverage of homicide tripled, even though the homicide rate went down."

National Criminal Justice Commission, February 1996

"When national news wants to excite viewers, it scours the nation for the day's most titillating crime, and broadcasts it everywhere. The result is a popular sense that rare and extreme crimes happen around every corner."

National Criminal Justice Commission, February 1996

"For example, since 1993, the homicide rate nationwide dropped by 20%. Yet since 1993, coverage of murders on the ABC, CBS, and NBC evening news increased by an astonishing 721%. As a result, in 1993 alone, the number of Americans ranking crime as the number one problem increased six fold."

Vincent Schiraldi (Justice Policy Institute Director) in the *Christian Science Monitor*, November 1997

QUICK—LET'S BUILD MORE PRISONS!

"Crime plummeted nationwide last year, for the fifth straight year, to its lowest levels since the government began keeping records a quarter-century ago, the Justice Department said," from which the executive director of the National Fraternal Order of Police naturally concluded that "Unless anti-crime efforts are intensified, we're going to be in for a horribly rude awakening."

Los Angeles Times, July 19, 1999

DON'T CONFUSE ME WITH THE FACTS, I'M ON A ROLL HERE

"Teen-agers account for the largest portion of all violent crime in America...They're the predators out there. They're the most violent criminals on the face of the earth."

U.S. Representative cum "House Manager" Bill McCollum (R-Fl), 1996

"...while juveniles accounted for about 19% of all violent crime arrests in 1994 (down from 23% in 1973), respondents to national polls believe that juveniles commit 43% of all violent crime."

Vincent Schiraldi (JPI Director) in the *Christian Science Monitor*, November 1997

"Ninety-two percent of the counties in America experienced one or no juvenile homicides in 1994."

Vincent Schiraldi (JPI Director) in the *Christian Science Monitor*, November 1997

"When Attorney General Janet Reno reported that violent juvenile crime had dropped a combined 11.9% over the past two years in the same week that the New Jersey and Mississippi (school shootings) occurred, her announcement received minimal media coverage, and was even ignored by her home town paper, the *Washington Post*."

Vincent Schiraldi (JPI Director) in the *Christian Science Monitor*, November 1997

WE'RE PLANNING FOR THE FUTURE

"Prison costs are rising faster than any other category of state spending. Increases in prison spending average twice as high as increases in education spending."

National Criminal Justice Commission, February 1996

"From 1984 to 1994, California built 21 prisons, and only one state university...the prison system realized a 209% increase in funding, compared to a 15% increase in state university funding."

The Justice Policy Institute, October 1996

"America spends 50% more incarcerating 1.2 million non-violent offenders than the entire $16.6 billion the federal government is currently spending on welfare programs that serve 8.5 million people."

Justice Policy Institute "The Punishing Decade," December 1999

WE CAN BARELY KEEP UP
WITH THE CASELOAD

All quotes in this section are taken from the FBI report, "Terrorism in the United States 1995" by the Terrorist Research and Analytical Center, National Security Division.

"Terrorists continued to threaten U.S. citizens and interests in the United States in 1995. The number of terrorist attacks here increased slightly over relatively low 1994 levels..."

Here we see the FBI subtly attempting to perpetuate an irrational fear of terrorist attacks against Americans before revealing that:

"Inside the United States, the FBI recorded one act of terrorism."

Which does indeed represent an increase over the "relatively low" number of acts recorded in 1994, since that year saw Americans victimized exactly 0 times. In fact, the two-year period in question yielded a grand total of just one solitary act of terrorism. This single act, it should be noted, was not the work of foreign agents, but of homegrown American psychopaths, trained by the U.S. military.

"The number of people killed in terrorist attacks in the United States increased sharply from previous years."

The FBI delivering another fear-inducing sound bite, before revealing that:

"Last year 168 people died in a single terrorist bombing in Oklahoma City. In 1994, no American in the United States died in a terrorist attack."

Here the FBI subtly acknowledges that no Americans had been killed in either year by foreign terrorist actions. This is not to say that such elements have not been busy, however. Indeed, the section of the report under the heading "Current Threat, International Terrorism," reproduced below *in its entirety*, makes abundantly clear the imminent threats facing the United States:

"Foreign terrorists viewed the United States as a priority target last year. Foreign terrorists and their supporters continued to live in and travel throughout this country."

And undoubtedly endangered countless American lives by doing so. The fact that the report was unable to document even a single act of international terrorism against Americans, and only one act of "domestic terrorism," did not in the least bit deter the authors from making the following hysterical pronouncements:

"Large-scale attacks designed to inflict mass casualties appear to be a new terrorist method in the United States."

"As in the past, it is likely that Americans at home and abroad will be the potential target of terrorists for the foreseeable future."

"...some terrorist supporters may be considering acts of revenge or blackmail."

"Some extremists and their followers here have demonstrated the ability to use advanced technology..."

"Extremists in the United States also continued a chilling trend by demonstrating interest in—and experimentation with—unconventional weapons."

WE CAN'T HELP YOU—WE'RE
SWAMPED OVER HERE, TOO

All quotes in this section are taken from the annual report by the U.S. State Department, "Patterns of Global Terrorism: 1998."

"The Secretary of State has designated seven countries as state sponsors of terrorism: Cuba, Iran, Iraq, Libya, North Korea, Sudan, and Syria."

In other words, the usual suspects. And just what nefarious pursuits, you may ask, have these outlaw nations been up to lately?

"There is no evidence of Libyan involvement in recent acts of international terrorism, however."

"There is no evidence of direct Syrian involvement in acts of international terrorism since 1986..."

"Cuba no longer supports armed struggle in Latin America or elsewhere."

However, we aren't quite ready yet to forgive and forget that...

"Although North Korea has not been linked definitively to any act of international terrorism since 1987, it continues to provide safehaven to terrorists who hijacked a Japanese airliner to North Korea in 1970."

The State Department report included several charts, a couple of which are reproduced here. These charts graphically illustrate the grave and increasing danger we as Americans face every single day in the heroic struggle against international terrorism.

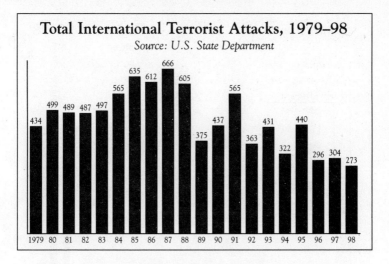

Total International Terrorist Attacks, 1979–98
Source: U.S. State Department

434, 499, 489, 487, 497, 565, 635, 612, 666, 605, 375, 437, 565, 363, 431, 322, 440, 296, 304, 273

1979 80 81 82 83 84 85 86 87 88 89 90 91 92 93 94 95 96 97 98

AT LEAST WE'RE MAKING
THE STREETS SAFER

"Five years after it was hailed as a major deterrent to crime, California's three-strike sentencing law has had no measurable effect on reducing violence…Crime has fallen at about the same rate in counties that aggressively enforce the three-strikes law as in those that do not, the study [by the Justice Policy Institute] found."

Los Angeles Times, **March 2, 1999**

"Justice Department statistics from mid-1998 show 74% of local jail inmates, 53% of state prison inmates and 88% of federal prisoners 'were imprisoned for offenses which involved neither harm nor the threat of harm to a victim'."

Los Angeles Times, **March 25, 1999**

"The report [by the Justice Policy Institute] estimates that at the end of 1998, there were…a national total of 1,185,458 nonviolent prisoners."

Los Angeles Times, **March 25, 1999**

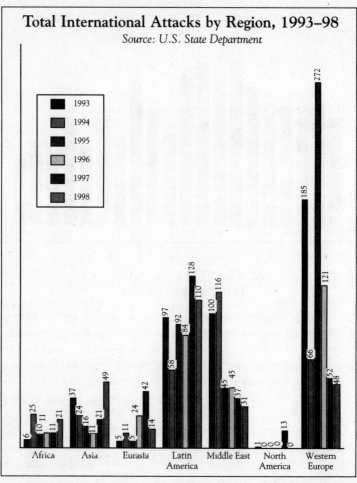

Total International Attacks by Region, 1993–98
Source: U.S. State Department

Legend: 1993, 1994, 1995, 1996, 1997, 1998

Africa: 6, 25, 10, 11, 11, 21
Asia: 37, 24, 16, 11, 21, 49
Eurasia: 5, 11, 5, 24, 42, 14
Latin America: 97, 58, 92, 84, 128, 110
Middle East: 100, 116, 45, 45, 37, 31
North America: 0, 0, 0, 0, 13, 0
Western Europe: 185, 66, 272, 121, 52, 48

"Prison has ceased to function as an effective deterrent in some communities because it is overused. Many young men regard time in prison as a rite of passage. As ever more young men are incarcerated, the ethos of the correctional facility—the accommodation to violence, erosion of sensitivity, generalized hostility—have come out to the streets and *made them more dangerous*."

National Criminal Justice Commission, February 1996 (emphasis added)

Section III

The Colorblind Society

CHAPTER 10

The American Apartheid

In many cities, about half of young African-American men are under the control of the criminal justice system. In Baltimore the figure is 56%; in D.C. it is 42%. In a single year in Los Angeles, one third of the young African-American men spend time behind bars.

— National Criminal Justice Commission, February 1996

America has come a long way in its 200+ year history in the area of race relations. Of course, considering that the country was founded on the principles of enslaving blacks and eradicating Native Americans, who had proven themselves much too resistant to enslavement, there was considerable improvement to be made. While the next chapter will look at the current situation of Native Americans, here we shall focus on the progress made by black Americans, specifically how race plays a key role in the machinations of the criminal justice system.

HE HAD A VERY SUSPICIOUS SKIN COLOR

"(B)lack drivers are targeted as suspected drug offenders on the basis of so-called 'race-based police profiles'—a practice so common that it is widely known as 'driving while black'."

**Amnesty International "United States of America—
Rights for All," October 1998**

"You may have noticed that many of the motorists pulled over on the side of the highway are black or hispanic. You may have attributed this to some kind of unspoken law-enforcement racism. You may be surprised to learn that *it's the result of a federal program*. Called Operation Pipeline."

Gary Webb "DWB" in *Esquire*, April 1998 (emphasis added)

"(Operation Pipeline is) run by hundreds of state and local police agencies across the country...with 301 police commands in forty-eight states...(with an) estimated twenty-seven thousand Operation Pipeline grads currently cruising the highways."

Gary Webb "DWB" in *Esquire*, April 1998

WE THINK WE'VE DEVELOPED A FOOL-PROOF SYSTEM FOR IDENTIFYING CRIMINALS

"Ron Hampton, a retired police officer and executive director of the National Black Police Association...told Amnesty International in 1998 that 'In a training video, every criminal portrayed is black.' "

**Amnesty International "United States of America—
Rights for All," October 1998**

THE WHITE MAN'S BURDEN

"The overwhelming majority of victims (of police abuse) in many areas are members of racial or ethnic minorities, while most police departments remain predominantly white."

**Amnesty International "United States of America—
Rights for All," October 1998**

"(O)nly 1% of the district attorneys in death penalty states in this country are black and only 1% are Hispanic. The remaining 97.5% are white, and almost all of them are male."

Death Penalty Information Center (DPIC) "The Death Penalty in Black & White," June 1998

WOULD THAT BE CONSIDERED A BLACKLIST?

"In Chambers County, Alabama, the prosecutor kept lists dividing prospective jurors into four categories: 'strong,' 'medium,' 'weak,' and 'black.'"

Death Penalty Information Center (DPIC) "The Death Penalty in Black & White," June 1998

WITH LIBERTY AND JUSTICE FOR ALL

"Overall, black and Hispanic inmates accounted for three-quarters of the total increase in Federal inmates…"

U.S. Department of Justice Bulletin NCJ170014, August 1998

"In 1996 the (incarceration) rate among black males totaled 3,098 prisoners per 100,000 residents, compared to 1,278 among Hispanic males and 370 among white males."

U.S. Department of Justice Bulletin NCJ170014, August 1998

"In 1997 the rate among black males in their late twenties reached 8,630 prisoners per 100,000 residents compared to 2,703 among Hispanic males and 868 among white males."

U.S. Department of Justice Bulletin NCJ175687, August 1999

"Approximately 80% of the young black men under age 35 have a criminal record."

National Criminal Justice Commission, February 1996

"… African Americans constitute 12% of the U.S. population, 13% of the drug using population, but an astonishing 74% of the people in prison for drug possession."

National Criminal Justice Commission, February 1996

"The racial impact of disenfranchisement laws was particularly egregious. Thirteen percent of African-American men—1.4 million—were disenfranchised…In seven states, one in four black men is permanently disenfranchised."

Human Rights Watch "World Report 1999, United States"

"Under current law, a seller of five grams of crack cocaine receives the same mandatory five-year prison term as a seller of 500 grams of powder cocaine. The U.S. Sentencing Commission has asked congress to reduce or eliminate the disparity, noting that a disproportionate number of African Americans are convicted of trafficking in crack…90 percent of the prisoners convicted for crack crimes are black, while most crack users are white."

The Washington Post, **October 21, 1997**

"In a study authored by Vincent Schiraldi, Christopher Davis and Richard Estes of the Center on Juvenile and Criminal Justice in San Francisco, the racial disparity in three strikes sentencing is clear. Blacks are sent to prison under the law 13 times more often than Whites."

Daniel Burton-Rose, Dan Pens, and Paul Wright, *The Celling of America*

"Overall, black men and women were at least 6 times more likely than whites to have been in prison at yearend 1997."

Press release for U.S. Department of Justice Bulletin NCJ175687, August 1999

I'VE NEVER SEEN THE WORD "BLACK" SPELLED LIKE THAT BEFORE

"The District of Columbia, a wholly *urban* jurisdiction, held 1,682 sentenced prisoners per 100,000 residents."

U.S. Department of Justice Bulletin NCJ170014, August 1998 (italics added)

SOME LIVES ARE JUST WORTH
MORE THAN OTHERS

"The gravity of the close connection between race and the death penalty is shown when compared to studies in other fields. Race is more likely to affect death sentencing than smoking affects the likelihood of dying from heart disease."

Death Penalty Information Center (DPIC) "The Death Penalty in Black & White," June 1998

"Blacks and whites in the U.S.A. are the victims of murder in almost equal numbers, yet 82 per cent of prisoners executed since 1977 were convicted of the murder of a white person…Blacks make up just 12 per cent of the country's population, but 42 per cent of the nation's condemned prisoners. In early 1998, of the 26 people under federal sentence of death (military and civilian), only five prisoners were white."

Amnesty International "United States of America— Rights for All," October 1998

"(L)ooking at the makeup of Kentucky's death row in 1996 revealed that 100% of the inmates were there for murdering a white victim, and none were there for the murder of a black victim, despite the fact that there have been over 1,000 African Americans murdered in Kentucky since the death penalty was reinstated."

Death Penalty Information Center (DPIC) "The Death Penalty in Black & White," June 1998

AT LEAST NOW WE GIVE THEM A TRIAL
BEFORE WE LYNCH THEM

" 'One of you two is gonna hang for this. Since you're the nigger, you're elected.' These words were spoken by a Texas police officer to Clarence Brandley, who was charged with the murder of a white high school girl. Brandley was later exonerated in 1990 after ten years on death row."

Death Penalty Information Center (DPIC) "The Death Penalty in Black & White," June 1998

"In preparing for the penalty phase of an African-American defendant's trial, a white judge in Florida said in open court: 'Since the nigger mom and dad are here anyway, why don't we go ahead and do the penalty phase today instead of having to subpoena them back at cost to the state.' Anthony Peek was sentenced to death and the sentence was upheld by the Florida Supreme Court in 1986 reviewing his claim of racial bias."

Death Penalty Information Center (DPIC) "The Death Penalty in Black & White," June 1998

"In the death penalty trial of Ramon Mata in Texas, the prosecutor and the defense attorney agreed to excuse all prospective minority race jurors, thereby ensuring an all white jury. The U.S. Court of Appeals for the Fifth Circuit found this to be harmless error."

Death Penalty Information Center (DPIC) "The Death Penalty in Black & White," June 1998

"In the Georgia trial of Wilburn Dobbs, a black man charged with the murder of a white man, both the judge and his attorney referred to Dobbs as a 'colored boy.' The defense attorney expressed his opinion that 'blacks are uneducated and would not make good teachers, but do make good basketball players,' and referred to the black community in Chattanooga as 'black boy jungle.' Dobbs was sentenced to death, and his conviction has been upheld by the Georgia courts."

Death Penalty Information Center (DPIC) "The Death Penalty in Black & White," June 1998

"William Henry Hance, a mentally-impaired black man, was sentenced to death in Georgia despite the fact that one of the jurors said she did not vote for death. The only black person on the jury stated that she had voted for a life sentence because of Hance's mental condition, but her vote was ignored. In the courtroom, she was intimidated against speaking out, but she later revealed her vote and the strong racial overtones in the jury room. Another juror signed an affidavit confirming the black juror's story, but Mr. Hance was executed anyhow in 1994."

Death Penalty Information Center (DPIC) "The Death Penalty in Black & White," June 1998

CHAPTER 11

Cowboys and Indians—The Continuing Saga

We must do what we can to recapture and to try to understand, in human terms, what it was that was crushed, what it was that was butchered. It is not enough merely to acknowledge that much was lost. So close to total was the incineration and carnage in the post-Columbian Americas, however, that of the tens of millions who were killed, few individual lives left sufficient traces for subsequent biographical representation.

— **David E. Stannard** *American Holocaust*, 1992

I don't feel we did wrong in taking this great country away from them...There were great numbers of people who needed new land, and the Indians were selfishly trying to keep it for themselves.

— **John Wayne, alleged actor and great American, in a *Playboy* interview, May 1971**

Americans have long been taught to deny the wholesale destruction of the Indian nations, cloaking it in terms such as "manifest destiny," or "westward expansion." The focus here is not on the early history of the United States, however, but on the 2.3 million Native Americans who remain in the United States today, as well as some of those in the remainder of the Americas. This is the story of a still-proud people who remain the most persecuted ethnic group in America today, while elsewhere in the Americas, far from the sheltered eyes of the U.S. citizenry, the slaughter of indigenous peoples continues unabated, just as it has for over 500 years.

STOP YOUR WHINING AND GET A JOB

"The Shannon County, S.D., reservation, home to 38,000 people, is a portrait of poverty. The median income of about $17,000 annually is about $20,000 below the national average, and 46.7% of the county's population lives in poverty. According to a Harvard University study, life expectancy here is 45, lower than that of any group in the United States. Nationwide, the unemployment rate has been below 5% for two years. Here it is 73%, a figure Clinton declared appalling."

Los Angeles Times, describing conditions on the
Pine Ridge Indian Reservation, July 8, 1999

SOME THINGS NEVER CHANGE

"At least 70% of the violent victimizations experienced by American Indians are committed by persons not of the same race— a substantially higher rate of interracial violence than experienced by white or black victims."

U.S. Department of Justice Report NCJ173386, February 1999

"American-Indian victims of violence were the most likely of all races of victims to indicate that the offender committed the offense while drinking."

U.S. Department of Justice Report NCJ173386, February 1999

WE DON'T DISCRIMINATE BY AGE OR SEX

"American Indians experience per capita rates of violence which are more than twice those of the U.S. resident population."

U.S. Department of Justice Report NCJ173386, February 1999

"Rates of violence in every age group are higher among American Indians than that of all races."

U.S. Department of Justice Report NCJ173386, February 1999

"Rates of violent victimization for both males and females are higher among American Indians than for all races."

U.S. Department of Justice Report NCJ173386, February 1999

THOUGH WE DO HAVE OUR FAVORITES

"The rate of violent crime experienced by American-Indian women is nearly 50% higher than that reported by black males."

U.S. Department of Justice Report NCJ173386, February 1999

"Nearly a third of all American-Indian victims of violence are between ages 18 and 24. This group of American Indians experienced the highest per capita rate of violence of any racial group considered by age—about 1 violence crime for every 4 persons of this age."

U.S. Department of Justice Report NCJ173386, February 1999

AND ALL THE REST WE JUST LOCK UP

"In 1997 about 16,000 American Indians were held in local jails—a rate of 1,083 per 100,000 adults, the highest of any racial group."

U.S. Department of Justice Report NCJ173386, February 1999

"On a per capita basis, American Indians had a rate of prison incarceration about 38% higher than the national rate."

U.S. Department of Justice Report NCJ173386, February 1999

JUST LIKE THE GOOD OLD DAYS

"A [UN-sponsored] truth commission report has concluded that the United States gave money and training to a Guatemalan military that committed 'acts of genocide' against the Mayan people during the most brutal armed conflict in Latin America, Guatemala's 36-year civil war [1960–1996]. The report of the independent Historical Clarification Commission, which was released on Thursday, contradicts years of official denial about the torture, kidnapping and execution of thousands of civilians in a war that the commission estimated killed more than 200,000 Guatemalans."

New York Times, February 26, 1999

"The massacres that eliminated entire Mayan villages are neither perfidious allegations nor figments of the imagination, but an authentic chapter in Guatemala's history."

Historical Clarification Commission "Guatemala,
Memory of Silence," February 1999

"…a time when 440 towns were being entirely destroyed by government troops, when almost 10,000 unarmed people were being killed or made to 'disappear' annually, and when more than 1,000,000 of Guatemala's approximately 4,000,000 natives were being displaced by the deliberate burning and wasting of their ancestral lands."

David E. Stannard *American Holocaust*, 1992

MAYBE IT WAS JUST A FEW "BAD APPLES"

"The results of our investigation demonstrate that in general, the excuse that midlevel commanders acted with a wide margin of autonomy—an excuse used in an attempt to justify what happened as 'excesses' and 'error' not ordered by superiors—is unsubstantiated and totally lacking any basis."

Christian Tomuschat, coordinator of the
Historical Clarification Commission

"The majority of human rights violations occurred with the knowledge or by order of the highest authorities of the state...The responsibility for a large part of these violations, with respect to the chain of military command as well as the political and administrative responsibility, reaches the highest levels of the army and successive governments..."

> Historical Clarification Commission "Guatemala,
> Memory of Silence," February 1999

"We found no evidence that Guatemala station was a 'rogue' station operating independently of control by its headquarters..."

> President's Intelligence Oversight Board "Report
> on the Guatemala Review," June 1995

I'M ALMOST POSITIVE IT WAS THEM, NOT US

"The commission has been able to establish that state forces and allied paramilitary groups were responsible for 93 percent of the documented violations, that the insurgent forces were responsible for 3 percent and that the remaining 4 percent of the cases include other authors..."

> Christian Tomuschat, coordinator of the
> Historical Clarification Commission

WHAT DO YOU MEAN BY 'HUMAN RIGHTS ABUSES'?

"On 9 December 1979, my 16-year-old brother Patrocino was captured and tortured for several days and then taken with twenty other young men to the square in Chajul...I was with my mother, and we saw Patrocino; he had had his tongue cut out and his toes cut off. The officer jackal made a speech. Every time he paused the soldiers beat the Indian prisoners...When he finished his ranting, the bodies of my brother and the other prisoners were swollen, bloody, unrecognizable...but they were still alive...They were thrown on the ground and drenched with gasoline. The soldiers set fire to the

wretched bodies with torches and the captain laughed like a hyena
and forced the inhabitants of Chajul to watch."

> Nobel Peace Prize winner Rigoberta Menchu Tum,
> as quoted by William Blum in *Killing Hope*

AND THEY SEEMED LIKE SUCH NICE GUYS

"The commission's investigations demonstrate that until the
mid-1980s, the United States Government and U.S. private companies exercised pressure to maintain the country's archaic and unjust
socio-economic structure. In addition, the United States
Government, through its constituent structures, including the
Central Intelligence Agency, lent direct and indirect support to
some illegal state operations."

> Christian Tomuschat, coordinator of the
> Historical Clarification Commission

"The commission listed the American training of the officer
corps in counter-insurgency techniques [at Ft. Benning] as a key factor 'which had a significant bearing on human rights violations during the armed confrontation.' "

> *New York Times*, February 26, 1999

"... maintaining influence in Guatemala required that the CIA
deal with some unsavory groups and individuals. The human rights
records of the Guatemalan security services were widely known to be
reprehensible, and although the CIA made efforts to improve the
conduct of the services...egregious human rights abuses did not
stop."

> President's Intelligence Oversight Board "Report
> on the Guatemala Review," June 1995

"In the course of our review, we found that several CIA assets
were credibly alleged to have ordered, planned, or participated in
serious human rights violations such as assassination, extrajudicial
execution, torture, or kidnapping while they were assets, and that

the CIA's Directorate of Operations (DO) headquarters was aware at the time of the allegations..."

> President's Intelligence Oversight Board "Report on the Guatemala Review," June 1995

AND IN CONCLUSION...

"Believing that the ends justified everything, the military and the state security forces blindly pursued the anti-Communist struggle, without respect for any legal principles or the most elemental ethical and religious values, and in this way completely lost any semblance of human morals..."

> Christian Tomuschat, coordinator of the Historical Clarification Commission

"As noted earlier, the IOB [Intelligence Oversight Board] believes that U.S. national interests, with respect to Guatemala and elsewhere, can in some cases justify relationships with assets and institutions with sordid or even criminal backgrounds."

> President's Intelligence Oversight Board "Report on the Guatemala Review," June 1995

"The Guatemalan Government's use of 'counter-terror' to combat insurgency...is indiscriminate, and we cannot rationalize that fact away...people are killed or disappear on the basis of simple accusations...The official squads are guilty of atrocities. Interrogations are brutal, torture is used and bodies are mutilated...We <u>have</u> condoned counter-terror; we may even in effect have encouraged or blessed it...We will stand before history unable to answer the accusations that we encouraged the Guatemalan Army to do these things."

> U.S. State Department Memorandum, March 29, 1968 (emphasis in original)

"Why would...the United States care about what is happening here? The reason is we are all one family and when one part of our family is not happy or suffers, we all suffer."

Secretary of State Madeleine Albright speaking to a group of children in Guatemala, quoted in the *Washington Post*, May 5, 1997

A POP QUIZ

"[T]he unlawful use of force or violence against persons or property to intimidate or coerce a government, the civilian population, or any segment thereof, in furtherance of political or social objectives."

The preceding statement is:

(a) the official FBI definition of terrorism, as per "Terrorism in the United States, 1995."

(b) a very accurate, though unofficial, description of CIA activities in foreign countries.

(c) both of the above.

Answer: c

"Only after the last tree has been cut down. Only after the last river has been poisoned. Only after the last fish has been caught. Only then you will find that money cannot be eaten."

An Anonymous Cree Indian

CHAPTER 12

Weird Science

It is better for all the world, if instead of waiting to execute degenerate offspring for crime, or to let them starve for their imbecility, society can prevent those who are manifestly unfit from continuing their kind…Three generations of imbeciles are enough.

— U.S. Supreme Court Justice Oliver Wendell Holmes, majority opinion in *Buck v. Bell*, 1925

Those who are physically and mentally unhealthy and unfit must not perpetuate their sufferings in the bodies of their children. Through educational means the state must teach individuals that illness is not a disgrace but a misfortune for which people are to be pitied, yet at the same time it is a crime and a disgrace to make this affliction the worse by passing it on to innocent creatures out of a merely egoistic yearning.

— Adolph Hitler *Mein Kampf*, 1925

Few people in the U.S. are aware that a truly "watershed achievement in biotechnology" occurred in November of 1998, according to British media sources, when "American Cell Technology (ACT), a leading, private biotechnology company, cloned the first human embryo and let it develop for twelve days before destroying it." This remarkable, though rather dubious, achievement was accomplished "using a cell from a man's leg and a cow's egg," and is believed to be only the first of many "human embryos [that] have been created and destroyed since November." Already there is a competitor in the field as well, as "another U.S. company, Geron, is also reported to be attempting to clone human embryos."[5] You might think that these would be newsworthy events, particularly in the country pursuing this research, but you would be mistaken. You might also think that human cloning was banned in the U.S., but again you would be mistaken. As it turns out, " 'Therapeutic cloning' of humans is illegal in Britain, though not in the United States,"[6] where it is also apparently not a matter for public debate.

These are not, mind you, actual people that are being created and destroyed, but "therapeutic clones." Therapeutic clones are grown, so the researchers tell us, as a source of tissue in an attempt to create human "stem cells," or "master cells," for use in transplantation and treatment of disease. So these are actually just collections of human embryonic tissue that roughly approximate the shape of an actual human. Besides this, the clones are only grown for 12 days and ACT's Director of Tissue Engineering assures us that "the embryo cannot be seen as a person before 14 days,"[7] that being the age at which the embryo would implant itself onto the wall of its mother's womb. Some people believe that life begins at conception, while others believe it begins at birth. But now we know that life actually begins at 14 days, and we know this because no less an authority than the Director of Tissue Engineering has said it is so. And, of course, there is no reason to doubt the company's sincere assurances that it actually is destroying all their little creations, though one *is* prone to wonder exactly whose leg it is that provided the cellular material being utilized to create these clones.

In other science and technology news, the U.S. Human Genome Project is proceeding along at a brisk pace, apparently much too fast for the media to keep up. The project, begun in 1990 and "coordinated by the U.S. Department of Energy and the National Institutes of Health," was originally projected to run through 2005, but "rapid technological advances have accelerated the project to an expected completion date of 2003." The goals of the research are to "identify all the estimated 80,000–100,000 genes in human DNA, determine the sequences of the 3 billion chemical bases that make up human DNA, store this information in databases, develop tools for data analysis, and address the ethical, legal, and social issues (ELSI) that may arise from the project."[8] In perusing the list of "Potential Benefits of Human Genome Project Research," proudly displayed on the project's official website, it's interesting to ponder what some of those ethical, legal, and social issues might be.

Under the heading of "Molecular Medicine," one of the benefits offered is the "earlier detection of genetic predisposition to disease," which is closely allied with another largely unstated goal of the project—the identification of a violence or aggression gene that would allow for early identification of future criminals and anti-social types. A similar benefit is found under the heading "Risk Assessment," where it is stated that this research can "reduce the likelihood of heritable mutations." All of this, of course, is hauntingly similar to various past projects and movements that have sought to provide scientific justification for the institution of official eugenics policies. After all, having identified all the "bad" genes swimming around in the national pool, it would be grossly irresponsible not to make every effort to remove them.

Another benefit listed under "Molecular Medicine" is the creation of "pharmacogenomics 'custom drugs,' " which are drugs tailored to particular genetic types. The problem with this avenue of research is that it bears a disconcerting similarity to the science of developing genetically specific biowarfare agents (i.e. biological agents designed to incapacitate or eliminate certain targeted ethnic groups). This is highlighted as another of the touted benefits of the project, under the heading of "Microbial Genomics," which is the potential for "protection from biological and chemical warfare." It bears noting here that research into protection from biowarfare is inseparable from research for conducting of biowarfare. They are, in essence, one and the same.

The Human Genome Project website does allude to some of these concerns in acknowledging that some ethical issues are "raised by the increased availability of genetic information," including: "genetic testing of an individual for a specific condition due to family history (prenatal, carrier, and presymptomatic testing) and population screening (newborn, premarital, and occupational)," "reproductive issues including informed consent for procedures, use of genetic information in decision making, and reproductive rights," and "how the resulting data may affect concepts of race and ethnicity; identify potential uses (or misuses) of genetic data in workplaces, schools, and courts." Notable also, both for its overtly racial overtones and for being incomprehensibly convoluted, is the statement that one of the project's goals for the period 1998–2003 is to "explore how racial, ethnic, and socio-economic factors affect the use, understanding, and interpretation of genetic information; the use of genetic services; and the development of policy."

Further benefits of this project can be found under the heading of "Agriculture, Livestock Breeding, and Bioprocessing," and include: "disease-, insect-, and drought-resistant crops," "healthier, more productive, disease-resistant farm animals," "biopesticides," and, a personal favorite, "edible vaccines incorporated into food products." And in what could perhaps be intended as comic relief, the researchers also claim to be seeking "new environmental cleanup uses for plants like tobacco," and further claim that "one researcher has genetically engineered tobacco plants in his laboratory to produce a bacterial enzyme that breaks down explosives such as TNT and dinitroglycerin. Waste that would take centuries to break down in the soil can be cleaned up by simply growing these special plants in the polluted area." Though these are clearly all major breakthroughs, particularly for all those currently struggling with the problem of what to do with the excessive build-up of TNT in their soil, they represent only a fraction of the ways in which your food is being genetically "improved" by the American scientific community.

The Environmental News Network informs us that if "in the past year you have topped off a sandwich with cheese, had a bowl of cereal or enjoyed a soft drink, chances are that you have eaten foods from genetically modified crops, according to university researchers. Over the past three years genetically enhanced crops have moved from the moral and ethical tables of debate to the dinner table."[9] Actually, in the interest of expediency, that business about the moral and ethical tables of debate appears to have been bypassed. This is quite likely due to the fact that a "1996 poll taken in Europe found that the more people know about genetic engineering, the less they like it."[10] American scientists were quick to realize that this little public relations problem could be easily solved within the U.S. by simply relieving the American people of the burden of debating such troubling issues. So while "consumers outside the U.S. have turned against GM (genetically modified) food,"[11] consumers inside the U.S. remain blissfully unaware.

Unaware, for instance, that "the use of genetically enhanced corn has increased from 400,000 acres in 1996 to three million acres in 1997 to an estimated 17 million acres planted in 1998." Unaware also that "in 1997, about 20 million acres of the soybeans planted in the United States were genetically enhanced" or that "about one-third of all dairy cattle in the United States are given bovine somatotropin, a hormone created through biotechnology, to increase milk production per cow."[12] Unaware even in the face of a prediction that "if the current rapid increase in the planting of GM crops continues, 85 to 90% of U.S. processed food will contain some element of genetic modification."[13] This perfect food, it is presumed, will be necessary to feed the perfect people.

Why are these issues of any significance? After all, haven't farmers been experimenting with genetics for centuries, producing various hybrids, seedless fruits and other such modified foods? While this is undeniably true, it is unlikely that any farmer would have come up with the idea to create "a potato genetically-modified with jellyfish genes which glows when it needs watering." This is a truly stunning breakthrough, solving the age-old problem that "farmers don't know how much water is needed—they just pour it on." And the best is yet to come: "future plans are to include slightly different fluorescent proteins which will report on the plants' nitrate, phosphate and sucrose status."[14]

Perhaps the most intriguing product to yet emerge from the food improvement labs is the so-called Terminator seed technology patented in March of 1998. This scientific milestone will replace old-fashioned, self-reproducing crop seeds with new and improved "seeds that will only work for one growing season, so farmers have to buy seed each time they plant."[15] This is necessary, assert the seed companies, to protect their new GM crops from being bootlegged, so to speak, by those who insist on harvesting seeds. To date, the seed cartels have "managed to control the "problem" of seed saving in this country by policing farmers. Monsanto requires that buyers of its Roundup Ready seeds agree to use them only once, and hires Pinkerton investigators to root out violators."[16] Once the new technology becomes universal, the seed police will become as obsolete as the archaic notion of self-perpetuating food crops.

The extent to which these disposable crops will replace their predecessors is evident in the fact that the "patent covers all seeds, both transgenic and everyday conventional varieties," as well as in the optimistic view of the inventors, who "believe it could work on all major crops." It is also apparent in the following statement by the president of Delta and Pine Land Company, who, together with the USDA, holds the patent: "We will make this as readily available to our direct competitors as we would to people working in crops that we have no interest in…In the spirit of trying to help everyone we will certainly be open to companies in other countries protecting their technology or their proprietary developments."[17] In other words, the day may soon come when an increasingly small group of multinational seed conglomerates control, quite literally, the world's food supply.

This is not necessarily a good thing. As Lawrence Busch, professor of sociology at Michigan State University notes: "The fact is that wars and civil disturbances and catastrophes of a natural variety occur. Those are the kinds of things that can wipe out seed supplies. If farmers can't plant the stuff that they harvest, and become totally dependent on this, you are really raising the ante on the possibility of mass starvation."[18] Indeed. There is also a legitimate fear that widespread use of this sterile seed technology will result in "greater amounts of identical crops (being) grown worldwide, increasing monocropping and further eroding agricultural biodiversity." The seed merchants, however, warn us that their seeds "may be our only hope for a withering environment and growing world population. These technologies, they say, may be our only way of *averting* mass starvation."[19]

What neither side in this rather limited debate have acknowledged is the vast military potential afforded by this technology. Simply put, this will ultimately put the food producing capability of the entire world securely in the hands of Western multinational corporations and the USDA. The coercive power that this will afford the United States in the forced promotion of its international agenda cannot possibly be overstated. In the age of super-sanctions, it will be possible, quite easy in fact, to literally starve entire continents into submission. The wonders of modern science.

"Up to now, living organisms have evolved very slowly, and new forms have had plenty of time to settle in. Now whole proteins will be transposed overnight into wholly new associations, with consequences no one can foretell, either for the host organism, or their neighbors...going ahead in this direction may be not only unwise, but dangerous. Potentially, it could breed new animal and plant diseases, new sources of cancer, novel epidemics."

Dr. George Wald, Nobel Laureate in Medicine 1967;
Higgins Professor of Biology, Harvard University

Section IV

Selling Death, Repression and a Little Cocaine

CHAPTER 13

Torture, Inc.

The U.S.A. has supplied arms, security equipment and training to governments and armed groups that have committed torture, political killings and other human rights abuses in countries around the world.

— **Amnesty International "United States of America— Rights for All," October 1998**

The United States has long been in the business of sponsoring brutally oppressive dictatorships around the globe, usually in the name of fighting communism and/or promoting democracy. The true purpose of these endeavors is the creation of easily exploitable labor and resource markets for the benefit of U.S. corporate interests. In this series of chapters, the focus is on the role America plays in supplying the means by which these regimes remain in power. This chapter takes a look at a particularly unsavory aspect of the international weapons bazaar, the trade in instruments of torture, and the training in how to use them.

WOULD YOU LIKE ANY BAMBOO SPLINTS TO GO WITH THAT?

"(F)rom September 1991 to December 1993 the U.S. Commerce Department had issued over 350 export licenses worth more than $27 million for: 'saps, thumb-cuffs, thumb-screws, leg-irons, shackles and handcuffs; specially designed implements of torture; strait jackets, plastic handcuffs, police helmets and shields.' These were issued for 57 countries, many of them with poor human rights records. In addition, over 2,000 licenses were issued for 105 countries under another export category, which combined electro-shock batons and cattle prods with shotguns and shells."

**Amnesty International "United States of America—
Rights for All," October 1998**

"(T)he U.S. Commerce Department had licensed the export of thousands of stun guns to Indonesia in 1993, in the face of persistent reports of electro-shock torture by Indonesian government agents... another State Department report on the use of U.S. military equipment was issued in July 1997. This admitted that Turkey's special units of paramilitary gendarmes and police—two of the forces most frequently accused of political killings, 'disappearances' and torture—were using M-16 and AR-15S assault rifles, M-203 grenade launchers and helicopters obtained from the U.S.A...In April 1998, a U.S. company was negotiating to sell 10,000 electro-shock weapons to the Turkish police, despite its long-standing and documented record of practising electro-shock torture."

**Amnesty International "United States of America—
Rights for All," October 1998**

IT DOESN'T DO ANY GOOD TO SELL THEM THE THUMB-SCREWS IF THEY DON'T KNOW HOW TO USE THEM

"U.S. Special Operations Forces trained 9,100 foreign soldiers in the 208 JCET [Joint Combined Exchange Training] exercises. Under the IMET [International Military and Education Training] program, U.S. forces trained 3,454 foreign forces, nearly all officers."

**Demilitarization for Democracy "Dictators or Democracies?
U.S. Arms Transfers and Military Training," April 1999**

"The School of the Americas (SOA), located in Fort Benning, Georgia, is the best known U.S. training facility, but it is only one of more than 150 centres in the U.S.A. and abroad where foreign officers are trained. A number of SOA 'alumni' have been implicated in gross human rights violations."

**Amnesty International "United States of America—
Rights for All," October 1998**

"Former Panamanian strongman and convicted drug trafficker Gen. Manuel Noriega graduated from the school. So did Roberto D'Aubuisson, architect of El Salvador's right-wing death squad network."

**Associated Press "School of the Americas=
School of the Assassins," May 2, 1998**

"D'Aubuisson has served as principal henchman for the wealthy landowners and as a coordinator of the right-wing death squads that have murdered several thousand suspected leftists and leftist sympathizers during the past year."

CIA Report to Vice President George Bush, March 18, 1981

"Nineteen of the 26 military officers that critics cited in the murder of six Jesuit priests and two women in El Salvador eight years ago were graduates of the School of the Americas."

**Associated Press "School of the Americas=
School of the Assassins," May 2, 1998**

"The nature of the Salvadoran army training was described by a deserter who received political asylum in Texas in 1990, despite the State Department's request that he be sent back to El Salvador... According to this deserter, draftees were made to kill dogs and vultures by biting their throats and twisting off their heads, and had to watch as soldiers tortured and killed suspected dissidents tearing out their fingernails, cutting off their heads, chopping their bodies to pieces and playing with the dismembered arms for fun."

Noam Chomsky, *What Uncle Sam Really Wants*

"...it was revealed recently that the school used manuals that included references to executions, torture and other human rights abuses."

**Associated Press "School of the Americas=
School of the Assassins," May 2, 1998**

"The U.S. government has acknowledged that parts of seven Spanish-language training manuals prepared and used by U.S. officials as recently as 1991 encouraged the use of murder, coercion and ill-treatment."

**Amnesty International "United States of America—
Rights for All," October 1998**

AND REMEMBER,
PLEASE DON'T TRY THIS AT HOME

"No assassination instruction should ever be written or recorded…The simplest local tools are often the most efficient means of assassination…anything hard, heavy and handy will suffice…The most efficient accident…is a fall of 75 feet or more onto a hard surface…Falls before trains and subway cars are usually effective, but require exact timing…assassinations can seldom be employed with a clear conscience. Persons who are morally squeamish should not attempt it."

"A Study of Assassination," a CIA training manual circa 1954

"It is possible to neutralize carefully selected and planned targets, such as court judges, mesta judges, police and state security officials, CDS chiefs, etc. For psychological purposes it is necessary to take extreme precautions…The mission to replace the individual should be followed by: Extensive explanation within the population affected of the reason why it was necessary for the good of the people."

**"Psychological Operations in Guerrilla Warfare,"
a Contra-era CIA Training Manual**

LET'S ALL BUILD OUR OWN
ARMIES AND PLAY WAR

"Globalization has given new characteristics to conflicts…In the power vacuum of the post-cold war era, military companies and mercenary armies began offering training to governments—and corporations. Accountable only to those who pay them, these hired military services pose a severe threat to human security."

United Nations Development Program
"Human Development Report 1999"

"Several U.S. companies with close links to the U.S. Department of Defense are now offering military training and other services that used to be provided only by governments. For instance, a U.S. company has received a substantial contract to help train and organize the armed forces of Bosnia-Herzegovina. In Saudi Arabia numerous U.S. companies are training every branch of the armed forces. In 1998, one U.S. company had over 1,000 employees in Saudi Arabia, mostly former U.S. army and special forces personnel, to 'modernize' the National Guard, a force responsible for internal security…Sometimes, both U.S. government and private military contractors have provided training and other support for foreign armed forces whose members are committing human rights abuses. This was the case for example in Rwanda from 1996 to 1998."

Amnesty International "United States of America—
Rights for All," October 1998

CHAPTER 14

Arms-R-Us

It is estimated that from 1989 to 1996 the U.S.A. sold more than $117 billion of arms, about 45 per cent of the global total ...

— Amnesty International "United States of America— Rights for All," October 1998

With Washington's share of the arms business jumping from 16 percent worldwide in 1988 to 63 percent today, U.S. arms dealers currently sell $10 billion in weapons to non-democratic governments each year.

— Project Censored "1998 Censored Foreign Policy News Stories"

In 1986 the United States accounted for 13 percent of worldwide arms exports, but today its share of the weapons market is an astounding 70 percent. Furthermore, 66 percent of all United States arms exports are to developing nations, many with fragile autocracies that are easily destabilized.

— British Medical Journal, October 14, 1995

In the wake of the dismantling of the former Soviet Union, the United States has become the preeminent arms dealer to the world, supplying fully two thirds of the world's military hardware. These weapons are sold to virtually any nation with an open checkbook, with no regard for the obscene human rights abuses enabled by these armaments in many of the nations that constitute America's best arms customers. Clearly, if the United States were truly interested in ending the international proliferation of arms and the easing of hostilities around the world, a unilateral freeze on international arms transfers would go a long way towards achieving that goal. To date, there has been no sign of such a move, with all signs pointing towards an increased proliferation of U.S. arms in the international marketplace, inevitably leading to greater international hostilities.

WE DON'T SELL THIS STUFF
TO JUST ANYONE

"[In 1998] military support was provided to 168 nations. Of these nations, 45 were developed nations and 123 were in the developing world."

Demilitarization for Democracy "Dictators or Democracies?
U.S. Arms Transfers and Military Training," April 1999

"From 1993 to 1997, the U.S. government sold, approved, or gave away $190 billion in weapons to virtually every nation on earth."

The Mojo Wire "U.S. Arms Sales: Arms Around the World"

I ALWAYS KNEW GEORGE BUSH
WAS A WIMP

"During Clinton's first year in office, U.S. arms sales more than doubled."

The Mojo Wire "U.S. Arms Sales: Arms Around the World"

"During Clinton's first year in office, U.S. foreign military aid soared to $36 billion, more than double what George Bush approved in 1992."

Project Censored "1998 Censored Foreign Policy News Stories"

WE WANT TO MAKE SURE WE BACK
THE WINNING TEAM

"Eritrea and Ethiopia, both non-democratic states, fought each other using U.S. arms and training."

**Demilitarization for Democracy "Dictators or Democracies?
U.S. Arms Transfers and Military Training," April 1999**

"[T]wo of America's biggest arms customers are Greece and Turkey, which have been threatening to go to war for decades over the tiny Mediterranean island of Cyprus."

***The Mojo Wire* "U.S. Arms Sales: Arms Around the World"**

IT GETS EXPENSIVE GUARDING OUR OILFIELDS

"Five nations received over $1 billion in U.S. military support in 1997: Taiwan ($6 billion), Saudi Arabia ($4.7 billion), Kuwait ($1.4 billion), Turkey ($1.3 billion), and Egypt ($1.2 billion)... Sixteen more received over $100 million..."

**Demilitarization for Democracy "Dictators or Democracies?
U.S. Arms Transfers and Military Training," April 1999**

AND WE'RE GOING TO
FIND OUT WHO'S DOING IT

"Of these 21 nations with transfers worth over $100 million, nearly all are receiving top-of-the-line U.S. air assets...In its brochure for the $80 billion F-22 next-generation fighter program, one of Lockheed Martin's key selling points was that 'sophisticated fighter airplanes and air defense systems are being sold around the world.'"

**Demilitarization for Democracy "Dictators or Democracies?
U.S. Arms Transfers and Military Training," April 1999**

"Nobody is doing a better job of arming the world than Lockheed-Martin; the company's portfolio of weapons and buyers is breathtaking…[Lockheed-Martin is] the world's largest arms maker with $28 billion in 1997 sales."

The Mojo Wire "U.S. Arms Sales: Arms Around the World"

THEY KEEP CATCHING UP WITH US—
IT'S THE DAMNEDEST THING

"Meanwhile, the Pentagon uses the presence of advanced U.S. weapons in foreign arsenals to justify increased new weapons spending."

Project Censored "1998 Censored Foreign Policy News Stories"

A FEW OF THEM CAN'T YET AFFORD
TO "BUY AMERICAN"

"Of the 53 armed forces in Africa, 41 (or 77 percent) received U.S. military training."

Demilitarization for Democracy "Dictators or Democracies?
U.S. Arms Transfers and Military Training," April 1999

"Of the 11 nations intervening in the civil war in the Congo in 1998, nine received U.S. arms and training in 1997."

Demilitarization for Democracy "Dictators or Democracies?
U.S. Arms Transfers and Military Training," April 1999

DOES ANYONE WANT THIS JUNK,
BEFORE WE TOSS IT?

"Since 1990 the U.S. government has given away more than $8 billion worth of 'surplus' equipment from U.S. military stocks, including 4,000 heavy tanks, 500 bombers and 200,000 light arms. Recipients in 1996 included Bahrain, Colombia, Egypt, Israel, Jordan, Mexico, Peru, and Turkey."

Amnesty International "United States of America-
Rights for All," October 1998

AT LEAST WE'RE KEEPING
AMERICANS WORKING

"According to the Pentagon, the defense industry laid off 795,000 American workers between 1992 and 1997."

The Mojo Wire **"U.S. Arms Sales: Arms Around the World"**

THEN AT LEAST WE'RE KEEPING
AMERICANS SAFE

"[T]he last five times U.S. troops were sent into conflict, they found themselves facing adversaries who had previously received U.S. weapons, military technology, or training."

Project Censored "1998 Censored Foreign Policy News Stories"

CHAPTER 15

Big Brother, Part 1—The New World Order

Numerous investigations and reports in the past decade have highlighted the extent to which the global arms trade nurtures and supports brutal and repressive regimes across the world. The industry and its participants have been put under the microscope by a number of parliamentary inquiries in Europe and North America. Without exception, these have uncovered a complex and profitable trade with few controls and with no ethical compass. Big Brother Incorporated is concerned with a parallel activity involving many companies involved in the arms trade. The international trade in surveillance technology (sometimes known as the Repression Trade) involves the manufacture and export of technologies of political control...Big Brother Incorporated is the first investigation ever conducted into this trade.

— **Privacy International "Big Brother Incorporated," November 1995**

The high-tech means of political control and repression are no longer just the stuff of science fiction novels and paranoid delusions. Rather, they constitute a booming international trade resulting in huge profits for some, and massive repression for many others. Most Americans are unaware that this technology even exists; even fewer are aware of the export of such technological systems or the ways in which they have been utilized. This chapter provides a brief overview of the newest aspect of the international arms trade, and America's role in it.

WE DON'T SELL THIS STUFF
TO JUST ANYONE, EITHER

"The report identifies the trade with such countries as Nigeria, China, Angola, Rwanda, Zambia and Indonesia. More than 80 British companies are involved, making the UK the world leader in this field. Other countries, in order of significance, are the United States, France, Israel, the Netherlands and Germany."

Privacy International "Big Brother Incorporated," November 1995

"The surveillance trade is almost indistinguishable from the arms trade. More than seventy per cent of companies manufacturing and exporting surveillance technology also export arms, chemical weapons, or military hardware."

Privacy International "Big Brother Incorporated," November 1995

"This technology is exported to virtually all countries with appalling human rights records."

Privacy International "Big Brother Incorporated," November 1995

GIVE ME A DOZEN OF EACH,
AND COULD YOU GIFT WRAP IT?

"Amongst the products involved are: telephone interception equipment, bugging devices, police and military information systems, ID cards, 'System X' telephone systems, communications logging systems, micro-cameras, parabolic microphones, automatic transcription systems, infrared scopes, night-vision equipment, advanced CCTV equipment, geographic information systems, vehicle-tracking technology, automated fingerprint systems, biometric technology, cellular intercept systems, computer intercept systems, crowd analysis and monitoring technology, [and] data matching programs…"

Privacy International "Big Brother Incorporated," November 1995

WE CAN'T CONTROL WHAT THEY DO WITH THIS STUFF AFTER WE SELL IT

"The technology described in this report makes possible mass surveillance of populations."

Privacy International "Big Brother Incorporated," November 1995

"Much of this technology is used to track the activities of dissidents, human rights activists, journalists, student leaders, minorities, trade union leaders, and political opponents."

Privacy International "Big Brother Incorporated," November 1995

AS LONG AS THERE IS NO POTENTIAL FOR ABUSE

"Rwanda will no longer distinguish between Hutus and Tutsis when it issues new identity cards, ending a practice that helped the Hutu militiamen to select their victims in last year's genocide… Hutu militiamen demanded the identity cards of civilians they stopped. If they were listed as members of the Tutsi minority, they were hacked to death or shot."

San Francisco Chronicle, June 9, 1995
[Note: in the Rwandan genocide, an estimated 800,000 persons were killed in just 100 days, in what is considered to be one of the most brutally efficient and well-organized acts of genocide ever committed.]

"In the 1980s, Israeli company Tadiram developed and exported the technology for the computerized death list used by the Guatemalan police."

Privacy International "Big Brother Incorporated," November 1995

"British computer firm ICL (International Computers Limited) provided the technological infrastructure to establish the South

African automated Passbook system, upon which much of the functioning of the Apartheid regime depended."

Privacy International "Big Brother Incorporated," November 1995

"In the late 1970s Security Systems International supplied security technology to Idi Amin's brutal regime in Uganda."

Privacy International "Big Brother Incorporated," November 1995

"The notorious human rights abuses in Indonesia—particularly those affecting East Timor—would not be possible without the strategic and technological support of Western companies. Amongst those companies supplying the Indonesian police and military with surveillance and targeting technology are Morpho Systems (France), De la Rue Printak (UK), EEV Night Vision (UK), ICL (UK), Marconi Radar and Control Systems (UK), Pyser (UK), Siemens Plessey Defense Systems (UK) Rockwell International Corporation (U.S.A.) and SWS Security (U.S.A.)."

Privacy International "Big Brother Incorporated," November 1995

"The Thailand Central Population Database and ID card system, developed by the U.S.-based Control Data Systems, involves sophisticated intelligence that has been used for political purposes by the Thai military. This integrated system creates an ID card, electronic fingerprint and facial image, and electronic data link involving the entire population. It spans most government agencies and is controlled by the powerful military/police-dominated Interior Ministry."

Privacy International "Big Brother Incorporated," November 1995

"...the notorious PROMIS surveillance software marketed throughout the world by the U.S. Justice Department has led to widespread fears about the creation of an *international* tracking system for individuals 'of interest.'"

Privacy International "Big Brother Incorporated," November 1995
(emphasis added)

CHAPTER 16

Crack Whores

> *While the Contra/drug question was not the primary focus of
> the investigation, the subcommittee uncovered considerable
> evidence relating to the Contra network which substantiated
> many of the initial allegations laid out before the committee
> in the spring of 1986. On the basis of this evidence, it is
> clear that individuals who provided support for the Contras
> were involved in drug trafficking, the supply network of the
> Contras was used by drug trafficking organizations, and ele-
> ments of the Contras themselves knowingly received financial
> and material assistance from drug traffickers. In each case,
> one or another agency of the U.S. government had informa-
> tion regarding the involvement either while it was occurring,
> or immediately thereafter.*

> — **Senate Committee Report on Drugs, Law
> Enforcement and Foreign Policy, 1989**

In 1996, the *San Jose Mercury News* ignited a firestorm of protest
when it ran a series of articles by investigative journalist Gary
Webb that seemed to provide substantial evidence of U.S. government complicity in drug trafficking. In an effort to circumvent a
congressional ban and provide illegal funding for the Nicaraguan
Contras, the CIA had, it was alleged, allowed and even assisted the
trafficking of massive amounts of cocaine into this country. Mr.
Webb and his paper were subsequently attacked by the holy trinity
of the "liberal" press, the *New York* and *Los Angeles Times*, and the

Washington Post. Was this a case of irresponsible, headline seeking journalism on the part of the *Mercury News*, or was it a case of extreme governmental corruption covered up by a compliant American press? More to the point, did the government actually work to create the crack cocaine explosion of the eighties and the attendant rise in urban violence, which it then used to enact a series of Draconian sentencing laws? A small portion of the more provocative evidence is presented here.

LT. COL. OLIVER NORTH: AMERICAN HERO

"As DEA officials testified last July before the House Judiciary Subcommittee on Crime, Lt. Col. Oliver North suggested to the DEA in June 1985 that $1.5 million in drug money carried aboard a plane...be provided to the Contras."

Senate Committee Report on Drugs, Law Enforcement and Foreign Policy, 1989

"[Contra leader] Pastora revealed as drug dealer."

Oliver North journal entry, March 26, 1984

"SETCO received funds for Contra supply operations from the Contra accounts established by Oliver North. U.S. law enforcement records state that SETCO was established by Honduran cocaine trafficker Juan Matta Ballesteros..."

Senate Committee Report on Drugs, Law Enforcement and Foreign Policy, 1989

"Wanted aircraft to go to Bolivia to pick up paste."
"Want aircraft to pick up 1,500 kilos."

Oliver North journal entries, both from July 9, 1984

"SETCO aviation is a corporation formed by American businessmen who are dealing with Matta and are smuggling narcotics into the United States."

U.S. Customs Service Investigative Report, file NOGGBDO30036, New Orleans, May 18, 1983

"Honduran DC-6 which is being used for runs out of New Orleans is probably being used for drug runs into U.S."

Oliver North journal entry, August 9, 1985

"One of the pilots selected to fly Contra supply missions for the FDN for SETCO was Frank Moss, who has been under investigation as an alleged drug trafficker since 1979. Moss has been investigated, although never indicted, for narcotics offenses by ten different law enforcement agencies."

Senate Committee Report on Drugs, Law Enforcement and Foreign Policy, 1989

"The State Department selected four companies owned and operated by narcotics traffickers to supply humanitarian assistance to the Contras. Ambassador Robert Duemling, Director of the Nicaraguan Humanitarian Assistance Organization...recalled that NHAO had been directed by Lt. Col. Oliver North to continue 'the existing arrangements of the resistance movement' in choosing contractors."

Senate Committee Report on Drugs, Law Enforcement and Foreign Policy, 1989

"$14M [million] to finance came from drugs."

Oliver North journal entry, July 12, 1985

On July 22, 1989, the Associated Press reported that Costa Rica, considered the most democratic of the notoriously undemocratic Central American nations, officially declared that it considered several high level U.S. officials to be drug traffickers, and that they would henceforth be barred from entering the country. The list included Lt. Col. Oliver North, Major General Richard Secord, and John Poindexter. The American press collectively ignored the AP release.

GEORGE'S MAN IN PANAMA

"...weapons for the Contras came from Panama on small planes carrying mixed loads which included drugs. The pilots unloaded the weapons, refueled, and headed north toward the U.S. with drugs."

Senate Committee Report on Drugs, Law Enforcement and Foreign Policy, 1989

"DIACSA's president, Alfredo Caballero, was under DEA investigation for cocaine trafficking and money laundering when the State Department chose the company to be an NHAO [Nicaraguan Humanitarian Assistance Organization] supplier. Caballero was at that time a business associate of Floyd Carlton— the pilot who flew cocaine for Panama's General Noriega. The laundering of money through DIACSA concealed the fact that some funds for the Contras were through deposits arranged by Lt. Col. Oliver North...the State Department was still doing business with DIACSA on its own behalf six months after the company's principals had been indicted."

Senate Committee Report on Drugs, Law Enforcement and Foreign Policy, 1989

"You are instructed that the United States has admitted for purposes of this trial the following facts to be true...In late August 1986, North reported to Admiral Poindexter that a representative of Panamanian leader Manuel Noriega had asked North to meet with him. Noriega's representative proposed that, in exchange for a promise from the U.S. government to help clean up Noriega's image and a commitment to lift the U.S. government ban on military sales to the Panamanian defense forces, Noriega would assassinate the Sandinista leadership for the U.S. government."

United States of America v. Oliver J. North, **Defendant: Criminal No. 88-0080 02—GAG**

WOULD YOU PREFER THE SNORTING OR NON-SNORTING SECTION?

"Gary Wayne Betzner, drug pilot who worked for convicted smuggler George Morales. Betzner testified that twice in 1984 he flew weapons for the Contras from the U.S. to northern Costa Rica and returned to the United States with loads of cocaine. Betzner is presently serving a lengthy prison term for drug smuggling."

Senate Committee Report on Drugs, Law Enforcement and Foreign Policy, 1989

"[T]he infrastructure used by the Contras and that used by drug traffickers was potentially interchangeable, even in a situation in which the U.S. government had itself established and maintained the airstrip involved."

**Senate Committee Report on Drugs, Law
Enforcement and Foreign Policy, 1989**

"Pilots who made combined Contra weapons/drug flights through the Southern Front included...Gerardo Duran, a Costa Rican pilot in the airplane parts supply business. Duran was convicted of narcotics trafficking in Costa Rica in 1987 and jailed."

**Senate Committee Report on Drugs, Law
Enforcement and Foreign Policy, 1989**

FORGET WHAT I SAID TWO YEARS AGO—OR WHY YOU SHOULDN'T TRUST THE *L.A. TIMES*

"If there was an eye to the storm, if there was a criminal mastermind behind crack's decade-long reign, if there was one outlaw capitalist most responsible for flooding Los Angeles' streets with mass-marketed cocaine, his name was Freeway Rick (Ross)...Ross did more than anyone else to democratize it, boosting volume, slashing prices and spreading disease on a scale never before conceived...South-Central's first millionaire crack lord...While most other dealers toiled at the bottom rungs of the market, his coast-to-coast conglomerate was selling more than 500,000 rocks a day, a staggering turnover that put the drug within reach of anyone with a few dollars."

**Jesse Katz in the *Los Angeles Times*, December 20, 1994, in
an article about Ricky Ross, who would later be identified by
Gary Webb as the man through whom the Contras funneled
literally tons of cocaine into South Central Los Angeles.**

"The crack epidemic in Los Angeles followed no blueprint or master plan. It was not orchestrated by the Contras or the CIA or any single drug ring. No one trafficker, even the kingpins who sold thousands of kilos and pocketed millions of dollars, ever came close to monopolizing the trade…How the crack epidemic reached that extreme, on some level, had nothing to do with Ross…[who was one of many] interchangeable characters…dwarfed by [other dealers]."

The same Jesse Katz in the same *Los Angeles Times*, October 20, 1996, shamelessly attempting to discredit Mr. Webb and his story, and succeeding primarily in discrediting himself and the *Times*.

CREATIVE DEFINITIONS OF A FREE PRESS—OR WHY YOU ALSO SHOULDN'T TRUST THE *WASHINGTON POST*

"We live in a dirty and dangerous world. There are some things the general public does not need to know and shouldn't. I believe democracy flourishes when the government can take legitimate steps to keep its secrets and when the press can decide whether to print what it knows."

***Washington Post* owner Katharine Graham speaking at CIA's Langley, Virginia headquarters in 1988, as reported in *Regardie's Magazine*, January 1990**

"How I Traveled Abroad on a CIA Subsidy."

Title of a confessional piece written by *Washington Post* reporter Walter Pincus in 1968; Pincus was one of the *Post*'s primary hatchet men in attempting to discredit Webb.

THE GREAT COMMUNICATOR

"…the moral equivalent of the Founding Fathers."

President Ronald Reagan referring to the Contras, on those occasions when he wasn't referring to them as "freedom fighters."

"With respect to (drug trafficking by) the Resistance Forces…it is not a couple of people. It is a lot of people…We knew that everybody around Pastora was involved in cocaine."

Iran-Contra testimony of CIA Central American Task Force Chief, August 5, 1987

READ MY LIPS

"I was out of the loop."

**Vice President George Bush, describing his
Iran-Contra role on numerous occasions.**

"Evidence obtained by the independent counsel establishes that the Iran-Contra affair was not an aberrational scheme carried out by a 'cabal of zealots' on the National Security Council staff…The evidence establishes that the central National Security Council operatives kept their superiors—including Reagan, Bush, Schultz, Weinberger and other high officials—informed of their efforts generally, if not in detail, and their superiors either condoned or turned a blind eye to them."

Lawrence Walsh, Independent Counsel for Iran-Contra, January 1994

"[There were] no benefits from the National Narcotics Border Interdiction System, directed by George Bush. In fact, the overall effect was to encourage supply…"

**U.S. General Accounting Office (GAO) Report, July 1985
(This report was released and subsequently suppressed following the
resignation of DEA head Francis Mullen, Jr. Mullen had referred
to Bush's efforts in fighting the "war on drugs" as "an intellectual
fraud" and "a liability rather than an asset.")**

YOUR HONOR, WE INTEND TO SHOW A PATTERN OF BEHAVIOR BY THE DEFENDANT

"Flying opium and heroin all over Indochina to serve the personal and entrepreneurial needs of the CIA's various military and political allies, ultimately turning numerous GIs into addicts. The operation was not a paragon of discretion. Heroin was refined in a laboratory located on the site of CIA headquarters in northern Laos. After a decade of American military intervention, Southeast Asia had become the source of 70 percent of the world's illicit opium and the major supplier of raw materials for America's booming heroin market."

**William Blum *Killing Hope*; see also Alfred W. McCoy
*The Politics of Heroin in Southeast Asia***

"Moujahedeen commanders inside Afghanistan personally controlled huge fields of opium poppies, the raw material from which heroin is refined. CIA-supplied trucks and mules, which had carried arms into Afghanistan, were used to transport some of the opium to the numerous laboratories along the Afghan-Pakistan border, whence many tons of heroin were processed with the cooperation of the Pakistani military. The output provided an estimated one-third to one-half of the heroin used annually in the United States and three-quarters of that used in Western Europe. In 1993, an official of the U.S. Drug Enforcement Administration called Afghanistan the new Columbia of the drug world."

William Blum *Killing Hope*

"Because the U.S. wanted to supply the Moujahedeen rebels in Afghanistan with stinger missiles and other military hardware it needed the full cooperation of Pakistan. By the mid-1980s, the CIA operation in Islamabad was one of the largest U.S. intelligence stations in the world. 'If BCCI is such an embarrassment to the U.S. that forthright investigations are not being pursued it has a lot to do with the blind eye the U.S. turned to the heroin trafficking in Pakistan' said a U.S. intelligence officer."

"The Dirtiest Bank of All," *Time*, **July 29, 1991**

THERE YOU GO AGAIN

"[Europol was] preparing a report for European interior and justice ministers on a connection between the KLA and Albanian drug gangs."

London Times, **March 24, 1999**

"Ethnic Albanians are now the most prominent group in the distribution of heroin in Western consumer countries."

Intelligence report by Germany's Federal Criminal Agency, in the *London Times*, **March 24, 1999**

"[C]ertain members of the ethnic Albanian community in the Serbian region of Kosovo have turned to drug trafficking in order to finance their separatist activities."

1995 U.S. Drug Enforcement Administration advisory, in the *San Francisco Chronicle*, May 5, 1999

"[T]he Balkan route is a principal thoroughfare for an illicit drug traffic worth $400 billion annually."

Interpol, quoted in the *San Francisco Chronicle*, May 5, 1999

DAMNED IF WE CAN FIGURE OUT WHY

"In the last two years, U.S. anti-narcotics aid to Colombia has tripled. But even as Washington has dispatched dollars and soldiers to the drug war, Colombian cocaine cultivation has soared 50%... While [President] Pastrana is expected to ask for yet more help, analysts worry that increased U.S. involvement in the drug war could actually be self-defeating, as the record of the recent past might indicate."

Los Angeles Times, August 8, 1999

"U.S. officials are investigating six to eight American Embassy employees and dependents in Columbia for possibly using the mission's postal system to smuggle illegal drugs or other contraband to the United States...The investigations began after the U.S. Army Criminal Investigation Division charged the wife of the Army officer in command of the U.S. military's counter-drug efforts in Columbia with illegally shipping cocaine to the U.S. via the seldom-inspected government mail system...U.S. officials described the investigations as particularly embarrassing because Columbia produces 80% of the world's cocaine and most of the $289 million in annual U.S. aid to the South American country goes to combat drug trafficking"

Los Angeles Times, August 14, 1999

In addition to Gary Webb's book, *Dark Alliance: The CIA, the Contras, and the Crack Cocaine Explosion*, two former DEA agents have also authored books accusing the CIA of complicity in the cocaine trade in Latin America. Michael Levine's book, *The Big White Lie: The CIA and the Cocaine/Crack Epidemic—An Undercover Odyssey*, covers the CIA's support for the cocaine coup in Bolivia in 1980. Celerino Castillo III has written about Contra cocaine trafficking in El Salvador in *Powderburns: Cocaine, Contras and the Drug War*.

Section V

The Prison
Industrial Complex

CHAPTER 17

The Incarceration of America

The U.S., which has 5% of the world population, will have a quarter of its prisoners in the year 2000.

— Justice Policy Institute "The Punishing Decade," December 1999

The United States now imprisons more people than any other country in the world – perhaps half a million more than Communist China.

— ***Atlantic Monthly*** **"The Prison-Industrial Complex," December 1998**

Our incarceration rate plays such a distorting role in the labor market, one study found that the U.S. unemployment rate would be 2% higher if prisoners and jail inmates were counted.

— Justice Policy Institute "The Punishing Decade," December 1999

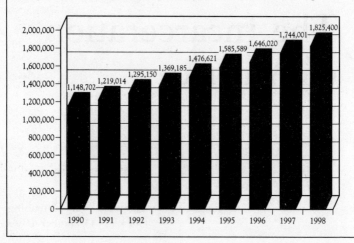

Total Number of Persons Incarcerated in the United States, 1990–1998

Data Source: U.S. Department of Justice Bulletin NCJ175687, August 1999

In this and the following chapters, the focus will be on the rise of what has been termed the prison-industrial complex. As the preceding chart graphically illustrates, the number of Americans taking up residence in one of the penal institutions that make up the U.S. prison complex is rapidly rising. The decade of the 1990s has seen the number of incarcerated individuals in this country nearly double, while politicians talk endlessly about getting ever tougher on crime. Already with the distinction of having the highest incarceration rate of any industrial democracy, the momentum is clearly towards building yet more prisons and depriving more Americans of their freedom. Is this due to the fact that American society breeds a higher rate of criminality than does other social systems? Or is it because the United States criminalizes more behavior than do other countries, exerting increasingly more control over its citizens' lives? These are clearly questions that the media feel are best left unasked and unanswered.

STILL PLENTY OF ROOM
LEFT AT THE INN

"On December 31, 1998, state prisons were operating at between 13% and 22% above capacity, while federal prisons were operating at 27% above capacity."

U.S. Department of Justice Bulletin NCJ175687, August 1999

"State, Federal, and local governments had to accommodate an additional 88,791 inmates per year (or the equivalent of 1,708 new inmates per week)."

U.S. Department of Justice Bulletin NCJ170014, August 1998

"Senator Jim Imhofe and Governor-elect Frank Keating are considering a proposal to ship Oklahoma inmates to Mexican prisons to ease overcrowding in state prisons..."

Daily Oklahoman **"Plan Reported to Ship Inmates to Mexico," December 23, 1994**

WE'RE AN EQUAL OPPORTUNITY
INCARCERATOR

"Incarceration rates have risen sharply among older age groups, women, and minorities."

U.S. Department of Justice Bulletin NCJ170014, August 1998

"During 1998 the number of women under the jurisdiction of state or federal prison authorities increased 6.5%...outpacing the rise in the number of men for the third consecutive year...Since 1990, the number of female prisoners has increased 92%."

U.S. Department of Justice Bulletin NCJ175687, August 1999

WE'RE LOCKING THEM UP
AS FAST AS WE CAN

"There are 11.5 million admissions to prison or jail annually. Every year, more people are arrested and jailed for a few days than the entire combined populations of Alaska, Delaware, Hawaii, Idaho, Maine, Montana, New Hampshire, North Dakota, Rhode Island, South Dakota, Vermont and Wyoming..."

National Criminal Justice Commission, February 1996

"A Justice Department study...showed the country's prison and jail population overall rose to about 1.8 million by the middle of last year, its highest level ever and double the number from 12 years before."

Los Angeles Times, **March 25, 1999**

"America incarcerates...five times as many people as Canada and seven times as many as most European democracies—despite the fact that we have similar overall rates of crime."

National Criminal Justice Commission, February 1996

"Crimes that in other countries would usually lead to community service, fines, or drug treatment—or would not be considered crimes at all—in the United States now lead to a prison term..."

Atlantic Monthly **"The Prison-Industrial Complex," December 1998**

IT'S WHAT WE LIKE TO CALL
A GROWTH INDUSTRY

"Throughout the first three quarters of this century the nation's incarceration rate remained relatively stable, at about 110 prison inmates for every 100,000 people. In the mid-1970s the rate began to climb, doubling in the 1980s and then again in the 1990s."

Atlantic Monthly **"The Prison-Industrial Complex," December 1998**

"[T]here were 668 inmates for every 100,000 U.S. residents as of June 1998, compared with 313 inmates per 100,000 people in 1985...The United States soon may surpass Russia as the country with the highest rate of incarceration."

Los Angeles Daily News, **March 15, 1999,**
citing a U.S. Justice Department study.

WELCOME TO CELLIFORNIA

"In 1977 the inmate population of California was 19,600. Today it is 159,000."

Atlantic Monthly **"The Prison-Industrial Complex," December 1998**

"California now has the biggest prison system in the Western industrialized world, a system 40 percent bigger than the Federal Bureau of Prisons. The state holds more inmates in its jails and prisons than do France, Great Britain, Germany, Japan, Singapore, and the Netherlands combined."

Atlantic Monthly **"The Prison-Industrial Complex," December 1998**

"[California's] penitentiary system, the most crowded in the country, has twice as many prisoners as it is designed to hold."

Los Angeles Times, **August 16, 1999**

"[California's] Department of Corrections is in the midst of a $5-billion prison building program—the nation's largest—that would increase the number of prison beds from 113,000 to almost 177,000."

Los Angeles Times, **August 16, 1999**

"For more than a century Folsom and San Quentin were the end of the line in California's penal system; they were the state's only maximum-security penitentiaries...From 1984 to 1994 California built eight new maximum-security (Level 4) facilities."

Atlantic Monthly **"The Prison-Industrial Complex," December 1998**

"The number of drug offenders imprisoned in the state today is more than twice the number of inmates imprisoned for all crimes in 1978."

Atlantic Monthly **"The Prison-Industrial Complex," December 1998**

THE POINT IS THAT WE'RE KEEPING
DANGEROUS CRIMINALS OFF THE STREET

"Eighty-four percent of the increase in admissions to prison since 1980 were non-violent offenders."

National Criminal Justice Commission, February 1996

"Eighty-seven percent of offenses nationwide are non-violent. Only 3% of all crime results in an injury. Homicide arrests constitute just 0.2% of all arrests in America."

National Criminal Justice Commission, February 1996

CHAPTER 18

Coddling the Criminals

Every day in prisons and jails across the U.S.A., the human rights of prisoners are violated. In many facilities, violence is endemic. In some cases, guards fail to stop inmates assaulting each other. In others, the guards are themselves the abusers, subjecting their victims to beatings and sexual abuse. Prisons and jails use mechanical, chemical and electro-shock methods of restraint that are cruel, degrading and sometimes life-threatening. The victims of abuse include pregnant women and the mentally ill.

— **Amnesty International "United States of America— Rights for All," October 1998**

Recent years have seen a marked shift in policy in U.S. prisons away from even the pretense of rehabilitation, with educational funding and other resources having been virtually eliminated. The focus now is clearly on punishment, with U.S. prisons finding themselves becoming nothing more than human warehouses. At the same time, significantly longer sentences, extreme overcrowding and greatly reduced prospects for parole for most inmates have created an incendiary mix in America's jails and prisons. Under these conditions, it is to be expected that increasingly brutal means will be required to maintain order.

WE DIDN'T HAVE ANY LIONS
TO FEED THEM TO

"Guards at Corcoran State Prison are alleged to have deliberately staged 'gladiator' fights between inmates and placed bets on the outcome. Between 1988 and 1994, seven prisoners were shot dead and dozens of others wounded when armed guards fired on them."

**Amnesty International "United States of America—
Rights for All," October 1998**

"In July, the state announced a new investigation into at least thirty-six serious and fatal shootings of Corcoran inmates."

Human Rights Watch "World Report 1999, United States"

"Forty-three more Corcoran prisoners were shot and seriously wounded, some paralyzed. After each killing, an internal review board would determine that the use of force had been necessary, that the shooting had been a 'good shoot,' and then things would carry on as usual."

**Richard Stratton "The Making of Bonecrusher,"
in *Esquire*, September 1999**

"It didn't matter to us. Who we killed, who was killed. It didn't matter, and everybody got cleared."

**Corcoran Prison guard Roscoe "Bonecrusher" Pondexter,
quoted in *Esquire*, September 1999**

AND THEY DIDN'T SMELL VERY GOOD EITHER

"Following a disturbance in Graham Unit, Arizona State Prison, in August 1995, more than 600 prisoners were forced by guards to remain handcuffed outdoors for 96 hours, and to defecate and urinate in their clothes. During daylight hours the heat was intense and many suffered serious sunburn, heat exhaustion and dehydration."

**Amnesty International "United States of America—
Rights for All," October 1998**

"Alabama Gov. Don Siegelman asked U.S. District Judge Myron Thompson for permission to resume handcuffing inmates to hitching posts in the hot sun when they refuse to work."

Los Angeles Times, June 14, 1999

WE'VE BEEN STUDYING THE TURKISH SYSTEM

"In many facilities, violence is endemic...The Justice Department and others have documented appalling conditions in dozens of jails: overflowing toilets and pipes; toxic and insanitary environments; prisoners forced to sleep on filthy floors without mattresses; cells infested with vermin and lacking ventilation...As local facilities have run out of room, a growing number of states have transported prisoners to out-of-state facilities, often thousands of miles away...When it ratified the ICCPR (in 1992) and the Convention against Torture (in 1994), the U.S.A. sought to limit the obligations imposed by the treaties [on treatment of prisoners]."

**Amnesty International "United States of America—
Rights for All," October 1998**

I DON'T REMEMBER READING
THAT IN THE BROCHURE

"Rape of prisoners by other inmates is reported to be alarmingly widespread."

**Amnesty International "United States of America—
Rights for All," October 1998**

"Prison staff often allowed or even tacitly encouraged sexual attacks by male prisoners."

Human Rights Watch "World Report 1999, United States"

THEY'RE GUILTY UNTIL PROVEN INNOCENT AROUND HERE

"Contrary to international standards, some jails do not segregate pre-trial detainees from convicted prisoners."

**Amnesty International "United States of America—
Rights for All," October 1998**

YOU ASKED FOR EQUALITY, AND NOW YOU'VE GOT IT

"In 1998 the Federal Bureau of Prisons agreed to pay three women $500,000 to settle a lawsuit in which the women claimed that they had been beaten, raped and sold by guards for sex with male inmates at a federal correctional facility in California."

**Amnesty International "United States of America—
Rights for All," October 1998**

"Reported sexual abuses by correctional staff include rape and other coerced sexual acts; staff routinely subjecting inmates to sexually offensive language; staff deliberately touching intimate parts of inmates' bodies during searches; and staff watching inmates who are undressed...U.S. correctional facilities employ both men and women to supervise prisoners of the opposite sex, allow them to undertake searches involving body contact, and permit them to be present where inmates are naked."

**Amnesty International "United States of America—
Rights for All," October 1998**

THANKS FOR CLEARING THAT UP

"The Santa Clara County, California, Board of Supervisors decided to commission a report...The county supervisors wanted to find out why jail detainees seemed to mysteriously die after 'tussling' with guards...The most startling conclusion highlighted in the report is that jail detainees and arrested suspects who 'inexplicably die' while in police custody may be victims of 'Sudden In-Custody Death Syndrome.' "

Daniel Burton-Rose, Dan Pens, and Paul
Wright *The Celling of America*

CHAPTER 19

Restraint, and Lack Thereof

The cruel use of restraints, resulting in unnecessary pain, injury or even death, is widespread in U.S. prisons and jails. Restraints are deliberately imposed as punishment, or used as a routine control measure rather than as an emergency response. Such practices breach international standards.

— **Amnesty International "United States of America— Rights for All," October 1998**

Another manifestation of the policy shift in America's prisons away from rehabilitation and towards punishment is the increasingly frequent use of restraints and electro-shock torture devices, as well as chemical sprays, to maintain order and to penalize those inmates who fail to show the proper deference to authority. As the United States' inmate population continues to grow, and their collective hopes for the future grow increasingly dim, yet more extreme forms of control will be required in the prison-industrial complex.

DON'T MAKE ME HAVE TO PUT YOU IN "THE CHAIR"

"Some of the most serious abuses in recent years have involved a steel-framed restraint chair which allows a prisoner to be immobilized with four-point restraints securing both arms and legs, and straps which can be tightened across the shoulders and chest."

**Amnesty International "United States of America—
Rights for All," October 1998**

"A directory called the Corrections Yellow Pages lists more than a thousand vendors. Among the items now being advertised for sale: a 'violent prisoner chair,' a sadomasochist's fantasy of belts and shackles attached to a metal frame, *with special accessories for juveniles*; B.O.S.S., a 'body orifice scanner,'...and a diverse line of razor wire, with trade names such as Maze, Supermaze, Detainer Hook Barb, and Silent Swordsman Barbed Tape."

Atlantic Monthly **"The Prison-Industrial Complex,"
December 1998 (emphasis added)**

NOW THAT'S WHAT I CALL A "TIME OUT"

"A lawsuit filed by the Justice Department in 1996 claimed that sheriff's deputies had routinely subjected inmates to 'cruel and unusual punishment, and physical and mental torture' by leaving them strapped in restraint chairs for extended periods in their own urine and excrement. According to the lawsuit, prisoners in the chair had their feet strapped behind them and their hands shackled behind or beneath their buttocks. Some prisoners had tape wrapped round their mouths and football helmets placed backwards on their heads. One 18-year-old inmate was reportedly held in the chair for eight days..."

**Amnesty International "United States of America—
Rights for All," October 1998**

SOMETIMES THE CHAIR ALONE ISN'T ENOUGH

"In June 1996 Scott Norberg died of asphyxia after being placed in a restraint chair with a towel wrapped over his face after he refused to leave his cell; before being strapped in the chair he was hit more than 20 times with an electric stun gun."

**Amnesty International "United States of America—
Rights for All," October 1998**

"The use of electro-shock stun technology in law enforcement raises concerns for the protection of human rights—not surprising, given that electricity has long been one of the favoured tools of the world's torturers."

Amnesty International "Cruelty in Control? The Stun Belt and Other Electro-Shock Equipment in Law Enforcement," June 1999

SOMETIMES WHEN WE GET BORED, WE'LL JUST PUSH A BUTTON AND THEN TRY TO GUESS WHO SHIT HIS PANTS

"(R)emote control electro-shock stun belts...which a guard can activate by the push of a button, inflict a powerful electric current, causing severe pain and instant incapacitation...and may cause him or her to defecate or urinate."

Amnesty International "United States of America—Rights for All," October 1998

"[T]he belt delivers a 50,000 volt, three to four milliampere shock which lasts eight seconds...The electro-shock cannot be stopped once activated."

Amnesty International "Cruelty in Control? The Stun Belt and Other Electro-Shock Equipment in Law Enforcement," June 1999

"Portable, easy to use, and with the potential to inflict severe pain without leaving substantial visible marks on the human body, electro-shock stun equipment is particularly open to abuse by unscrupulous law enforcement officials."

Amnesty International "Cruelty in Control? The Stun Belt and Other Electro-Shock Equipment in Law Enforcement," June 1999

"Children, at least those tried as adults, are not exempt from being made to wear the stun belt."

Amnesty International "Cruelty in Control? The Stun Belt and Other Electro-Shock Equipment in Law Enforcement," June 1999

"...at least 20 state prison systems now authorize stun belts, which first came into use in the U.S. law enforcement community about five years ago...Kaufman (president of the belt's primary manufacturer, Stun Tech, Inc.) said that his firm's stun-belt business is increasing at a rate of about 20% a year and that Amnesty International's research on the increased popularity of the belts appears solid."

Los Angeles Times, June 9, 1999

WE COULDN'T GET "THE CHAIR" INTO THE COURTROOM

"The belt...is also used on prisoners during judicial hearings, in breach of international standards on the treatment of prisoners."

Amnesty International "United States of America—Rights for All," October 1998

"Stun Tech's promotional literature has listed possible uses of the stun belt thus: 'for transportation details, inmate control, transportation of *mentally ill people* and in courtrooms."

Amnesty International "Cruelty in Control? The Stun Belt and Other Electro-Shock Equipment in Law Enforcement," June 1999 (emphasis in original)

CHAPTER 20

The Human Warehouse

When you arrive at Upstate, the guards will confiscate most of your possessions…All you'll have to entertain you are a pen, paper, and your cell mate…you won't be leaving your cell at all. Food trays arrive through a slot in the door, and there's a shower in the corner that's carefully regulated to spew lukewarm water three times a week…A guard in a central tower will control your access to the outside world. Each day, the officer will unlock your back door by flipping a switch in the control room. Now is the time for "recreation"…At Upstate, "rec time" means 60 minutes by yourself in the outdoor cage attached to the rear of your cell. It's about half the size of your cell, just big enough to do jumping jacks.

— **Village Voice "The Supermax Solution,"**
May 19–25, 1999

A s the two previous chapters have noted, the "get tough on crime" agenda has resulted in a marked shift in philosophy in this country concerning the role of prisons towards one of punishment and containment. Nowhere can this trend be more clearly seen than in the proliferation of so called "supermaximum security," or supermax facilities. Here we take a peek inside what could well be the prototype for the human kennels of the future.

I SUPPOSE I COULD JUST
CLIMB THE WALLS ALL DAY AGAIN

"Since the late 1980s the federal system and an increasing number of states have built so-called supermaximum security (or 'supermax') facilities...In 1997, 36 states and the federal government were reported to operate at least 57 supermax facilities...Many more are under construction...The cells tend to have solid steel doors rather than bars, cutting off sound and visual contact with others, including prisoners in the next cell. No televisions, radios, newspapers or books are allowed in the most restricted units."

**Amnesty International "United States of America—
Rights for All," October 1998**

OR MAYBE I'LL START WORKING
ON MY FECES SCULPTURE

"Prisoners typically spend between 22 and 24 hours a day confined to small, solitary cells in which they eat, sleep and defecate...In some units, cells have no windows to the outside and prisoners have little or no access to natural light or fresh air, in violation of international standards."

**Amnesty International "United States of America—
Rights for All," October 1998**

TIME REALLY FLIES IN HERE

"In the Maximum Control Complex (MCC) at Westville, Indiana, prisoners were not allowed to wear watches or ask the time..."

**Amnesty International "United States of America—
Rights for All," October 1998**

"Some prisoners may spend years in supermax units. In 22 jurisdictions, it is possible for inmates to complete their sentences in supermax housing and be released to the community without any transitional stage."

Amnesty International "United States of America—Rights for All," October 1998

THEY GOT EXACTLY WHAT THEY DESERVED

"Prisoners may be assigned for long periods to the supermax unit in Wabash, Indiana, for relatively minor disciplinary infractions, such as insolence towards staff, and the period may be extended for transgressions committed there. Others have reportedly been moved to supermax units because of overcrowding or because they have complained about prison conditions...[Some women] have alleged that they were assigned, or threatened with assignment, to the supermax unit if they complained about sexual abuse by guards."

Amnesty International "United States of America—Rights for All," October 1998

THE OPINIONS EXPRESSED IN THIS BOOK ARE NOT NECESSARILY THOSE OF THE AUTHOR

"Some prisoners have reportedly been put in supermax units because of their political affiliations..."

Amnesty International "United States of America—Rights for All," October 1998

SPENDING QUALITY TIME TOGETHER

"Severe overcrowding led New York's prison officials to begin double-celling inmates in 1995. This practice started with the least violent inmates, and it never applied to prisoners who had...been sentenced to 23 hours a day in their cells. Until now. Upstate will enforce a new form of punishment by locking pairs of men together, all day, in 14-by-8 1/2-foot cells. At this two-story prison, 1500 inmates will be crammed together, watched over by 800 surveillance cameras and 370 guards."

Village Voice "The Supermax Solution," May 19–25, 1999

"[T]his policy (double-celling) has an ominous history. Pelican Bay State Prison in California is in the midst of eliminating this practice because 10 prisoners have killed their cell mates in the last few years."

Village Voice "The Supermax Solution," May 19–25, 1999

CHAPTER 21

If You Build It, They Will Come

While arrests and convictions are steadily on the rise, profits are to be made—profits from crime. Get in on the ground floor of this booming industry now!

— From a brochure for a conference on prison privatization held December 1996 in Dallas, Texas.

In order to cut costs, states have increasingly contracted out to private firms the management of facilities as well as services such as health care. As a result, incarceration has become one of the fastest growing businesses in the U.S.A., generating large profits...

— Amnesty International "United States of America— Rights for All," October 1998

The idea of private prisons was greeted with enthusiasm during the Reagan and Bush Administrations...The Clinton Administration, however, has done far more than its Republican predecessors to legitimize private prisons.

— Atlantic Monthly "The Prison-Industrial Complex," December 1998

The privatization of the prison industry, creating an entirely new American industry dependent upon filling prison cells to make a profit, has been accompanied by the equally disturbing trend towards the use of prison labor forces by private industry. On the bright side, these parallel trends should stop some of the siphoning off of jobs out of the country and into third world slave-labor markets, while still allowing American corporations to post record-breaking profits. Of course sustaining those profits will require a steady flow of new prisoners, creating a self-sustaining system that, once built, will become a permanent part of the landscape.

WE'RE TRYING TO MAKE A PROFIT HERE

"…approximately 100,000 adults were confined in 142 privately owned prisons and jails nationwide."

Human Rights Watch "World Report 1999, United States"

"Many experts believe that the involvement of private companies increases the likelihood of inmates being abused and subjected to poor conditions. They suggest that private companies have a stronger interest in cutting costs, which can lead to less investment in staffing, training, health care, educational or rehabilitation programs, and even food. Such fears are borne out by serious complaints about conditions in privately run facilities in a number of states."

Amnesty International "United States of America— Rights for All," October 1998

"States failed to enact laws setting appropriate standards and regulatory mechanisms for private prisons, signed weak contracts, undertook insufficient monitoring and tolerated prolonged substandard conditions."

Human Rights Watch "World Report 1999, United States"

"In August 1997 a videotape, *apparently compiled for training purposes*, showed guards in a privately run section of Brazoria County

Detention Center, Texas, kicking and beating inmates, coaxing dogs to bite prisoners and using stun guns."

> **Amnesty International "United States of America—
> Rights for All," October 1998 (emphasis added)**

IT'S A GOOD THING WE HAVE PLENTY OF CRIMINALS

"To be profitable, private prison firms must ensure that prisons are not only built but also filled. Industry experts say a 90 to 95 per cent capacity rate is needed to guarantee the hefty rates of return needed to lure investors."

> *CounterPunch* **"America's Private Gulag," January 1997**

ALL ABOARD!

"The private prison business is most entrenched at the state level but is expanding into the federal prison system as well. Last year Attorney General Janet Reno announced that five of seven new federal prisons being built will be run by the private sector."

> *CounterPunch* **"America's Private Gulag," January 1997**

"In addition to the companies that directly manage America's prisons, many other firms are getting a piece of the private prison action. American Express has invested millions of dollars in private prison construction in Oklahoma and General Electric has helped finance construction in Tennessee. Goldman Sachs & Co., Merrill Lynch, Smith Barney, among other Wall Street firms, have made huge sums by underwriting prison construction with the sale of tax-exempt bonds, this now a thriving $2.3 billion industry."

> *CounterPunch* **"America's Private Gulag," January 1997**

"The prison-industrial complex now includes some of the nation's largest architecture and construction firms, Wall Street investment banks that handle prison bond issues and invest in private prisons, plumbing-supply companies, food-service companies, health-care companies, companies that sell everything from bullet-resistant security cameras to padded cells available in a 'vast color selection'."

Atlantic Monthly "The Prison-Industrial Complex," December 1998

IT WORKED FOR I.G. FARBEN,
FOR A WHILE AT LEAST

"Convicted kidnapper Dino Navarrete…earns 45 cents an hour making blue work shirts in a medium-security prison near Monterey, California. After deductions, he earns about $60 for an entire month of nine-hour days…Navarrete was surprised to learn that…California, along with Oregon, was doing exactly what the U.S. has been lambasting China for—exporting prison-made goods."

Covert Action Quarterly #54, Fall 1995

Some of the country's largest and most profitable corporations have quietly begun to use prison labor forces, at wages up to 80% below the national minimum wage. Among those reportedly contracting to employ prisoners, either directly or through their subsidiaries: AT&T, Bank of America, Boeing, Chevron, Costco, Dell Computers, Eddie Bauer, IBM, Konica Business Machines, Microsoft, Starbucks, Texas Instruments, TWA, and US West.

**Michael Moore *Downsize This*, Daniel Burton-Rose,
et. al. *The Celling of America*, and *Covert
Action Quarterly* #54, Fall 1995**

"In a revealing comment, Oregon State Representative Kevin Mannix argues that corporations should cut deals with prison systems just as Nike shoes does with the Indonesian government. Nike subcontractors there pay workers $1.20 per day. 'We propose that [Nike] take a look at their transportation costs and their labor costs,' says Mannix. 'We could offer [competitive] prison inmate labor' in Oregon."

Covert Action Quarterly #54, Fall 1995

"Neither slavery or involuntary servitude, *except as punishment for crimes whereof the party shall have been duly convicted*, shall exist within the United States, or any place subject to their jurisdiction."

Thirteenth Amendment to the United States Constitution (emphasis added)

IMPRISONING NOT JUST AMERICA, BUT THE WORLD

"U.S. companies have also been expanding abroad. The big three (Corrections Corporation of America, Wackenhut Corrections Corporation, and Esmor) have facilities in Australia, England and Puerto Rico and are now looking at opportunities in Europe, Canada, Brazil, Mexico and China."

CounterPunch **"America's Private Gulag," January 1997**

"Wackenhut Corrections is now under contract to operate Doncaster prison, in England; three prisons in Australia; and a prison in Scotland. It is actively seeking prison contracts in South Africa."

Atlantic Monthly **"The Prison-Industrial Complex," December 1998**

Section VI

Everything is Under Control

CHAPTER 22

Big Brother, Part 2—The Homecoming

New technologies which were originally conceived for the defense and intelligence sectors have after the cold war rapidly spread into the law enforcement and private sectors...there has been a political shift in targeting in recent years. Instead of investigating crime (which is reactive) law enforcement agencies are increasingly tracking certain social classes and races of people living in red-lined areas before crime is committed...

— Scientific and Technological Options Assessment (STOA) "An Appraisal of the Technologies of Political Control," September 1998

People don't quite get it yet...soon there will be computer files of facial images, and when you walk in (a building), your face will be instantly scanned by the computer, so you'll be recognized by name. All these devices can be linked together and allow police to spy in real time...

— Marc Rotenberg, head of the Electronic Privacy Information Center, quoted in *Rolling Stone* #819, August 1999

I n chapter 16, an overview was provided of the international trade in surveillance technology and how it has been utilized by repressive foreign regimes, as well as what the end results of that utilization have been. In this chapter, the focus will be on how various facets of this technology are increasingly being applied here in America, for the most part without even the illusion of public debate. The extent to which our personal privacy has already been eroded will probably come as something of a shock to most readers. More shocking are the prospects for the future, as this technology flourishes in the vacuum of public awareness.

WE KNOW WHO YOU ARE

"A small New Hampshire company that wants to build a national database of driver's license photographs received nearly $1.5 million in federal funds and technical assistance from the U.S. Secret Service last year, according to documents and interviews with officials involved in the project...As the company lobbied to gain access to motor vehicle files, officials apparently told few people about its ties to the Secret Service or the money it received from Congress. State legislators, motor vehicle administrators and others who worked with the company said in interviews they had no inkling that federal officials might be involved."

Washington Post, **February 18, 1999**

"The revolution in urban surveillance will reach the next generation of control once reliable face recognition comes in. In fact, an American company Software and Systems has trialed a system in London which can scan crowds and match faces against a database of images held in a remote computer." [Such as the above mentioned driver's license photo database, for example.]

STOA "An Appraisal of the Technologies of Political Control," September 1998

"Technologically, facial recognition is fairly cutting edge, but the concept behind it is really quite simple. Each person's facial features from the eyes to the jaw are shaped and positioned in subtly different ways. The software is trained to measure spatial relationships among facial features and to convert that information into a mathematical map of the face...While humans might be easily fooled by changed facial hair or glasses, the computer sees through those things...Likewise, an aging suspect is not a problem, because even as a person sprouts wrinkles or gains weight, the basic facial features don't change all that much."

Congressional Quarterly, Inc. **"The Digital Mugshot"**

"A new security system being developed in Britain can identify individuals by the unique way in which they walk. Unlike faces and irises, someone's gait can be spotted from a great distance with low-resolution cameras and so be observed from just about any angle. It is also very difficult to mask..."

New Scientist **"Watch How You Walk, You May Incriminate Yourself," December 4, 1999**

"This week, the FBI launched its National Crime Information Center 2000, replacing the old computer network...Local police can now take a single fingerprint from a suspect at a roadside arrest and find out in minutes from a new FBI computerized national crime data system whether that person is wanted..."

Los Angeles Times, **July 16, 1999**

"[W]hen DNA sequencing technologies progress further, direct characterization of very large DNA segments, and possibly even whole genomes, will become feasible and practical and will allow precise individual identification."

The Human Genome Project website

"[The] FBI and each of the 50 states are building an interlinked computerized database that already has a backlog of 1 million blood and tissue samples taken from crime scenes and convicted offenders...Attorney General Janet Reno is calling for the DNA fingerprinting of everyone arrested in the United States, potentially as many as 15 million people a year."

Paul DeRienzo and Joan Moossy "Gene Cops,"
In These Times, **December 1999**

WE KNOW WHERE YOU ARE

"Similarly, Vehicle Recognition Systems have been developed which can identify a car number plate then track the car around a city using a computerised geographic information system. Such systems are now commercially available."

**STOA "An Appraisal of the Technologies of
Political Control," September 1998**

"Receivers for Global Positioning System satellites will become a feature in every new car's navigation system, perhaps allowing a system 'hacker' to track your whereabouts to a centimeter's accuracy."

San Jose Mercury News, **July 1, 1996**

"In the skies above cities will soon appear some tiny, pilotless aircraft that might be mistaken for model airplanes. They're not. Inside will be high-resolution cameras that can make out small objects from hundreds of yards, infrared detectors that can see in the dark—and maybe even chemical sensors that can pinpoint drugs in the area...And they're just one small ripple in the wave of the future. Across the country police agencies are extending the long arm of the law by using eerily invasive high technology to speed the work of catching crooks, tracking stolen goods, and snooping on suspected wrongdoers."

The Wall Street Journal, **December 12, 1990**

"In Japan, cell phones are used to track the precise whereabouts of their users (the software lets you punch in someone's phone number and gives back his location, even the floor he's on). A locational capacity is coming soon to American cell phones by order of the Federal Communications Commission."

**William Greider "The Cyberscare Of '99," in
Rolling Stone #819, August 1999**

"Law enforcement officials with a judge's order will be able to determine the general location of wireless phone callers under new standards adopted Friday by the Federal Communications Commission. Privacy advocates criticized the action, charging that the FCC has compromised people's privacy by allowing law enforcement officials to use mobile phones as tracking devices."

San Jose Mercury News, **August 28, 1999**

"The official anti-missile [SDI] scheme calls for a constellation of surveillance satellites (Brilliant Eyes), watching for fiery rocket plumes, the telltale indicator of a enemy launch...In the unofficial version, much of which has been invented in Livermore, the Eyes will be equipped with radar, lasers, telescopes, antennae and sensors to allow military commanders to see practically every square foot of Earth—and analyze that information instantly."

San Jose Mercury News, **August 2, 1992**

WE KNOW WHO YOU'RE TALKING TO

"Without debate or notice, U.S. lawmakers...approved a proposal [House Resolution 3694] long sought by the FBI that would dramatically expand wiretapping authority—an idea Congress openly rejected three years ago. The provision, allowing law enforcement agencies more easily to tap any telephone used by or near a targeted individual instead of getting authorization to tap specific phones, was added to the Intelligence Authorization conference report during a closed-door meeting..."

Reuters, October 8, 1998
(HR 3694 was signed into law by President Clinton
October 20, 1999, becoming Public Law #105-272.[2])

"[T]he 1994 Communications Assistance in Law Enforcement Act (CALEA)...gave the FBI extraordinary power to demand that telephone companies rebuild their networks to make wiretapping easier."

The CATO Institute

"The Federal Communications Commission on Friday approved a series of telephone industry standards aimed at bringing law enforcement wiretaps into the Digital Age...The FCC will require telecommunications companies to provide six of nine new surveillance capabilities that have been on the 'wish list' of the Justice Department and the Federal Bureau of Investigation...phone companies will have to equip their cellular towers to allow court-authorized traces of cellular phone calls. They also will have to equip their services so that wiretaps can be made of conference calls...The FCC order implements the 1994 Communications Assistance for Law Enforcement Act."

Los Angeles Times, **August 28, 1999**

"Australia has become the first country openly to admit that it takes part in a global electronic surveillance system...The disclosure is made today...by Martin Brady, director of the Defence Signals Directorate in Canberra. Mr. Brady's decision to break ranks and officially admit the existence of a hitherto unacknowledged spying organisation called UKUSA is likely to irritate his British and American counterparts...Together with the giant American National Security Agency (NSA) and its Canadian, British, and New Zealand counterparts, DSD operates a network of giant, highly automated tracking stations that illicitly pick up commercial satellite communications and examine every fax, telex, e-mail, phone call, or computer data message that the satellites carry...Information is also fed into the Echelon system from taps on the Internet, and by means of monitoring pods which are placed on undersea cables. Since 1971, the U.S. has used specially converted nuclear submarines to attach tapping pods to deep underwater cables around the world."

The Age **"Careful, They Might Hear You," May 23, 1999**

WE KNOW ALL ABOUT YOU

"The federal agencies that govern the nation's banks and thrifts have proposed regulations that, if approved, would force financial institutions to report to police any suspicious—but perfectly legal— activity in their customers' accounts...The 'Know Your Customer' program, as it is called, by the four federal agencies that proposed it last winter, would force banks and thrifts to monitor their customers' transactions and financial patterns. If a transaction deviates from that pattern—such as a large deposit or withdrawal—the financial institutions would be required to alert federal authorities."

Los Angeles Daily News, March 4, 1999

"Federal officials will soon begin collecting personal information about millions of homebound patients—including details about their mental stability, financial status and living arrangements—in an effort to improve service in the home health care industry."

Los Angeles Times, March 11, 1999

"Individual medical records, *including patients' genetic information*, could be disclosed by health insurers to credit card companies and other financial institutions under legislation overwhelmingly approved Thursday by the House."

Los Angeles Times, July 2, 1999 (emphasis added)

"Scores of California banks, thrifts, credit unions and life insurers have begun turning over confidential information about their customers—including account balances and Social Security numbers—to state officials in an effort to comply with a new federal law designed to catch parents who fail to pay child support...about half of the participating institutions are taking advantage of a provision that enables them to simply hand over the names and account balances of *all their customers...*"

Los Angeles Times, July 16, 1999 (emphasis added)

"In addition to detailing its plan (Compliance 2000), the IRS gave notice that 'this system is exempt from the notification, access and contest provisions of the Privacy Act (1974).' This means that the IRS doesn't need permission to dig up information, doesn't need to show it to you and doesn't need to correct the information even if it's wrong."

New York Post, October 16, 1995

"A sweeping measure by the European Union aimed at protecting its citizens' privacy in the digital age sets strict rules for companies that handle European consumers' personal data...The measures underscore long-standing differences between the patchwork approach to privacy protections in the United States and more aggressive European policies shaped by a history of abuses dating back to Nazi Germany…This piecemeal approach helps to explain why the United States is the biggest market in the world for…personal data."

Los Angeles Times, March 6, 1999

"Twenty-four hours a day, Acxiom electronically gathers and sorts information about 196 million Americans. Credit card transactions and magazine subscriptions. Telephone numbers and real estate records. Car registrations and fishing licenses. Consumer surveys and demographic details."

Washington Post, March 8, 1998, explaining the functioning of the nation's largest data warehouse.

"In a flash, data warehouses can assemble electronic dossiers that give marketers, insurers and in some cases law enforcement a stunningly clear look into your needs, lifestyle and spending habits."

Washington Post, March 8, 1998

"The number of data warehouses…now exceeds 1,000, a tenfold increase in five years…Analysts at the META Group estimate that the money spent on building and maintaining data warehouses will increase from about $2 billion in 1995 to more than $10 billion in the year 2000."

Washington Post, March 8, 1998

DON'T LEAVE HOME WITHOUT IT, OR ELSE!

"There is much to do here, but I was just saying to Ted [Kennedy] before he left, a hearing like this fifteen years ago would have torn the building down. And here we are today, just a bunch of us, kind of sitting around and no media, no nothing. This is fine with me. I get tired of them on this issue."

Senator Alan Simpson, at May 10, 1996 Congressional Subcommittee meeting on national ID law.

"[The national ID card will have a] magnetic strip on it in which the bearer's unique voice, retina pattern, or fingerprint is digitally encoded."

Senator Dianne Feinstein, author of the national ID law

"[A]fter October 1, 2000, Federal agencies may only accept as proof of identity driver's licenses that conform to standards developed by the Secretary of the Treasury."

Public Law 104-208, Part B, Title IV, Section 656

MAYBE I'LL HOLD OFF ON
THOSE UPGRADES AFTER ALL

"The Microsoft Corporation moved to defuse a potentially explosive privacy issue today, saying it would modify a feature of its Windows 98 operating system that has been quietly used to create a vast data base of personal information about computer users...[which] could result in the ability to track a single user and the documents he created across vast computer networks...subpoenas might allow authorities to gain access to information that would otherwise remain private and unavailable."

New York Times, March 7, 1999

"[T]he serial number embedded in each new Pentium III will enable online marketers, even governments, to track computer users' movements on the Internet..."

New York Times, February 19, 1999
(Intel officials claim that this feature is no longer active on their chips, a stance they took only after the ID feature was publicized in the mainstream media.)

THE INFORMATION SUPER-SPYWAY

"It would be beneficial for Internet service providers to capture and retain Caller ID data on persons accessing ISP lines. The capturing of Caller ID data will greatly assist law enforcement..."

FBI Director Louis Freeh, speaking before a Senate Subcommittee, 1998.

"The Clinton Administration has developed a plan for an extensive computer monitoring system, overseen by the Federal Bureau of Investigation...The plan calls for the creation of a Federal

Intrusion Detection Network, or Fidnet, and specifies that the data it collects will be gathered at the National Infrastructure Protection Center, an interagency task force housed at the Federal Bureau of Investigation...it would put a new and powerful tool into the hands of the FBI."

New York Times, July 28, 1999

"The Justice Department wants to make it easier for law enforcement authorities to obtain search warrants to secretly enter a suspect's home or office and disable security on personal computers as a prelude to a wiretap or further search, according to documents and interviews with Clinton administration officials. In a request set to go to Capitol Hill, the Justice Department will ask lawmakers to authorize covert action..."

Los Angeles Times, August 20, 1999

THE PROVERBIAL "FLY ON THE WALL"

"Researchers at the University of California at Berkeley are building a minuscule robot...Known affectionately as 'robofly,' the gadget is exactly what the name implies: a flying robot about the size of a housefly...'The potential application of a robot based on a fly might be, in an urban environment, clandestine surveillance and reconnaissance,' said Teresa McMullen of the Office of Naval Research. In other words, that fly might be a spy."

San Francisco Chronicle, November 2, 1999

YOU CAN RUN, BUT YOU CAN'T HIDE

"Three high-tech labs are in the final stages of developing a new form of radar device that can see through walls by broadcasting radio signals across broad bands of the spectrum to pinpoint a hidden suspect...[Raytheon] promises MARS [Motion and Ranging Sensor] will spot a lurking fugitive 100 feet away. That kind of range— achieved by adapting military missile guidance technology—is enough to find someone hiding two stories up inside a building…Raytheon's Motion and Ranging Sensor system scientists at Georgia Tech are working on [another] system—a lightweight through-the-wall radar system that fits inside a flashlight…We're trying to reach every policeman on the beat,' said Gene Greneker, the scientist at the Georgia Tech Research Institute who developed the radar flashlight…The demand for these products is high, and the National Institute of Justice has placed through-the-wall surveillance at the top of its scientific funding priority list for the past two years."

Sightings "New X-Ray Vision Will Let Cops See
Through Walls," July 21, 1999

WE KNOW WHAT YOU'RE DOING
BEFORE YOU EVEN DO IT

"[W]hether for good or bad, surveillance machines are going to get smarter. They're already starting to recognise people's faces in the street, and systems that spot abnormal behavior will not be far behind…a sophisticated visual security system that predicts when a crime is about to be committed…was developed by Steve Maybank at the University of Reading and David Hogg at the University of Leeds…Once connected to such intelligent systems, closed-circuit television (CCTV) will shift from being a mainly passive device for gathering evidence after a crime, to a tool for crime prevention…[The system works by detecting any behaviors that deviate from the 'normal' range of human behavior:] the computer recognises them as patterns. If anyone deviates from these patterns, the system sounds the alarm…it spots any abnormal behavior."

New Scientist "Warning! Strange Behaviour," December 11, 1999

"This is a very dangerous step towards a total control society… The push to conformity will be extraordinary."

Privacy International Director Simon Davies
in *New Scientist*, December 11, 1999

CHAPTER 23

Building a Better Police State

At the same time, FBI and Department of Justice officials participated in numerous national and international conferences...These meetings were designed to increase cooperation among U.S. police agencies—as well as among foreign security services—to form a united law enforcement front against terrorism inside the United States and around the world.

> — The FBI's Terrorist Research and Analytical Center, National Security Division, "Terrorism in the United States 1995" (emphasis added)

BUILDING A BETTER POLICE STATE— A CHECKLIST

X (1) Create a climate of fear among the people by exploiting urban crime and alleged terrorist activities so as to fool them into willingly surrendering their constitutional rights and protections.

X (2) Authorize the police to use military-style helicopters to patrol the night skies at low altitudes, and to possess fully-automatic weaponry and armored personnel carriers, as well as the occasional grenade launcher.

X (3) Attach catchy name brand labels, like "Three Strikes" and "10-20-Life," to Draconian sentencing legislation to insure popular support and passage.

X (4) To avoid the possibility of criminals getting off on "technicalities," pass congressional legislation decimating the exclusionary rule. (1984)

X (5) Allow police officers to obtain search warrants based solely on the word of an informant, who needn't even be named, and unsupported by probable cause. ("Snitch," PBS *Frontline*)

X (6) Pass federal forfeiture statutes allowing the state to seize the property of alleged drug dealers without due process, while pretending that this practice isn't blatantly unconstitutional. (1990)

X (7) Allow federal agents to wiretap any phone calls for up to 48 hours without the bother of obtaining a court order. (Anti-Terrorism and Effective Death Penalty Act of 1996)

X (8) Enact "mandatory minimum" sentencing laws, thereby shifting discretionary power out of judges' hands and into the hands of overzealous prosecutors. (1986 Anti-Drug Abuse Act)

X (9) Allow these same federal prosecutors to make extensive use of informants to garner stunningly high conviction rates, even in the absence of any physical evidence. ("Snitch," PBS *Frontline*)

X (10) Remove the jury from the sentencing process in federal cases to such an extent that jurors are not informed of the fate awaiting those they have just convicted. ("Snitch," PBS *Frontline*)

X (11) Have the courts turn a mostly blind eye while federal prosecutors routinely violate "discovery" procedures by withholding material from defense attorneys.

X (12) Offer no parole in federal cases. ("Snitch," PBS *Frontline*)

X (13) Strictly limit the amount of "good time" a prisoner can earn toward early release, which combined with no possibility of parole guarantees that a prisoner can reduce his sentence only by becoming a snitch. (See #9 above.)

X (14) Have the president issue a call, in his 1999 State of the Union address, for the application of "high technology" to the country's police forces, as well as for the creation of a new domestic "anti-terrorist" police force.

X (15) Shortly thereafter, have the president call for the creation of a new military post, "Commander in Chief of the Continental United States," despite the fact that the principle of *posse comitatus* prohibits the use of the U.S. military for domestic law enforcement.

X (16) Have the U.S. 4th Circuit Court of Appeals issue a ruling that directly attacks the protections afforded by *Miranda v. Arizona*, granting a suspect the right to remain silent, the right to an attorney, etc.. (February 1999)

X (17) Punish anyone arrogant enough to plead innocent to a federal charge by explicitly encoding it into law that fighting a federal charge will result in a longer prison term than pleading guilty to the very same charge. ("Snitch," PBS *Frontline*)

X (18) Conduct terrorist response exercises across the country involving various local, state and federal police and military units to facilitate the creation of a singular, unified domestic paramilitary police force.

X (19) Approve congressional legislation calling for a national ID card.

X (20) Issue a Supreme Court ruling allowing the police to pull over and search any vehicle, on the pretext of making a routine traffic stop. (*Whren v. U.S.*, No. 95-5841)

X (21) Issue additional ruling allowing the police, during such "pretext stops," to search the belongings of any and all occupants of the vehicle. (*Wyoming v. Houghton*, No. 98-184)

X (22) "[Reshape] the federal appeals courts, creating a two-level justice system in which tens of thousands of appeals receive limited reviews," specifically those of defendants of color and/or limited financial means. (*New York Times*, March 14, 1999)

X (23) Have congress amend the "False Statements Statute," granting to prosecutors "the extraordinary authority...to manufacture crimes...(resulting in) government generation of a crime when the underlying suspected wrongdoing is or has become nonpunishable." (Supreme Court Justice Ruth Bader Ginsburg, 1996)

X (24) Begin a full scale militarization of borders: "On a 242-181 vote, the House endorsed an amendment offered by Rep. James A. Trafficant Jr. (D-Ohio) to authorize the Defense Department, at the request of the attorney general or treasury secretary, to dispatch troops to assist the Immigration and Naturalization Service and the Customs Service in their border drug interdiction and counter-terrorism activities." (*Los Angeles Times*, June 11, 1999)

THIS STUFF IS SELLING LIKE HOT CAKES

"Many cold war military suppliers are converting to civilian law enforcement. The Department of Justice, the CIA and the Pentagon are quietly taking an active and coordinated role in marketing defense-related technologies to law enforcement agencies."

National Criminal Justice Commission, February 1996

"Throughout the nation, paramilitary, SWAT or tactical policing—that is, law enforcement that uses the equipment, training, rhetoric and group tactics of war—is on the rise. According to a study by sociologist Peter Kraska, the nation has more than 30,000 such heavily armed, militarily trained police units...Between 1995 and 1997 the DOD (United States Department of Defense) gave local police departments more than 3,800 M-16 automatic assault rifles, 2,185 M-14 semiautomatic rifles, 73 M-79 grenade launchers and 112 armored personnel carriers—1.2 million pieces of military hardware in 1997 alone."

The Nation "SWAT Nation," May 31, 1999

"The Pentagon and the Justice Department have agreed on the outlines of a plan to share state-of-the-art military technology with civilian law-enforcement agencies, including exotic 'non-lethal' weapons such as sticky foam for immobilizing criminals and giant snares for trapping cars. Other items that will be evaluated for combating crime include infrared surveillance gear, sonar devices for pinpointing the origin of gunfire and digital information systems that could permit instantaneous transmission of photographs of crime suspects to police in the street…"

San Jose Mercury News, March 23, 1994

YOU JUST CAN'T BE TOO CAREFUL OUT THERE

"On one such evening, three squads of ten police officers in combat boots, black jumpsuits, military helmets and bulletproof vests lock and load their Heckler & Koch MP-54 submachine guns (the same weapons used by the elite Navy SEALs) and fan out through the neighborhood…Since 1994 the VCSU has patrolled this city's have-not suburbs in full military gear, with automatic assault rifles at the ready. Backed by two helicopters with infrared scopes and an Army-surplus armored personnel carrier, the unit is also equipped with attack dogs, smoke bombs, tear gas, pepper spray, metal clubs and less-than-lethal 'blunt trauma' projectiles."

The Nation "SWAT Nation," May 31, 1999, describing the routine activities of Fresno, California's Violent Crime Suppression Unit (VCSU).

CHAPTER 24

Fear of FEMA

Since its founding in 1979, FEMA's mission has been clear: to reduce loss of life and property and protect our nation's critical infrastructure from all types of hazards through a comprehensive, risk-based, emergency management program of mitigation, preparedness, response and recovery.

— **FEMA website**

Most Americans are aware of the Federal Emergency Management Agency, if at all, only in its capacity as the handler of natural disasters, such as earthquakes and tornadoes. In this capacity, FEMA likes to present itself as the knight in shining armor, arriving just in time to save the suffering victims from the earth's destructive powers. Unfortunately, the agency has a far more disturbing function, one that was first made public in October of 1984 by columnist Jack Anderson, when he reported that FEMA had drafted "standby legislation (to) suspend the constitution and the Bill of Rights...and generally clamp Americans in a totalitarian vise." Since that time, a few scattered reports make it possible to piece together how this agency acquired such extraordinary power, and under what circumstances it could wield it.

According to one account, "On October 30, 1969 President Richard Nixon issued Executive Order 11490, 'Assigning Emergency Preparedness Functions to Federal Departments and Agencies,' which consolidated some 21 operative Executive Orders and two Defense Mobilization Orders issued between 1951 and

1966 on a variety of emergency preparedness matters."[20] This Executive Order made a significant change to Executive Order 11051, signed by President Kennedy on October 2, 1962, which declared that "national preparedness must be achieved...as may be required to deal with increases in international tension with limited war, or with general war including attack upon the United States." While this order appeared to target emergency preparations at countering foreign threats, Nixon's order began: "Whereas our national security is dependent upon our ability to assure continuity of government, at every level, in any national emergency type situation that might conceivably confront the nation," thereby leaving open the possibility that virtually *anything* could be considered a national emergency.

It is notable that virtually all of FEMA's powers were created by Presidential Executive Order, a notably undemocratic form of legislation. Executive Orders become law as soon as they are recorded; there is no Congressional or judicial review, and certainly no public approval or even awareness. The next order came in 1976 from Nixon-appointed President Gerald Ford, who "ordered the Federal Emergency Preparedness Agency (FEPA, predecessor to FEMA) to develop plans to establish government control of the mechanisms of production and distribution of energy sources, wages and salaries, credit and the flow of money in American financial institutions in any (heretofore undefined) 'national emergency.' This Executive Order (EO 11921) also indicated that, when a state of emergency is declared by the President, congress could not review the matter for a period of six months."[21]

So already by 1976 we have a federal agency acquiring quite extraordinary powers to circumvent the Constitution. Next up to bat was President Jimmy Carter, who "signed Executive Order 12148 which created the Federal Emergency Management Agency (FEMA) to replace the Federal Emergency Preparedness Agency. This Presidential Directive mandated an interface between the Department of Defense (DOD) and FEMA for civil defense planning and funding."[22] Here we see a foreshadowing of an unholy alliance that would more fully develop under the watch of the next White House occupant, President Ronald Reagan, who "from

February to July of 1982...signed a series of National Security Decision Directives (NSDD)—presidential decisions on national security objectives—on civil defense policy and emergency mobilization preparedness."[23]

Some of the details of this emergency mobilization preparedness were to come to light in a remarkable story that appeared in the *Miami Herald*. It seems that Lt. Col. Oliver North, in the early days of the Reagan Administration, "widened his assignment to cover national crisis contingency planning. In that capacity he became involved with the controversial national crisis plan drafted by the Federal Emergency Management Agency. From 1982 to 1984, North assisted FEMA, the U.S. government's chief national crisis-management unit, in revising contingency plans for dealing with nuclear war, insurrection or massive military mobilization." Colonel North, last seen facilitating the sale of crack cocaine to inner city youth, helped draft a "secret contingency plan that called for suspension of the Constitution, turning control of the United States over to FEMA, appointment of military commanders to run state and local governments and declaration of martial law during a national crisis. The plan did not define national crisis, but it was understood to be nuclear war, violent and widespread internal dissent or national opposition against a military invasion abroad."[24]

True to form for North and his associates, the plan for martial law had decidedly racist overtones. As reported by the *Herald*, which had possession of the smoking gun documentation: "The martial law portions of the plan were outlined in a June 30, 1982, memo by (FEMA Director) Guiffrida's deputy for national preparedness programs, John Brinkerhoff. A copy of the memo was obtained by the *Herald*. The scenario outlined in the Brinkerhoff memo resembled somewhat a paper Guiffrida had written in 1970 at the Army War College in Carlisle, Pa., in which he advocated martial law in case of a national uprising by black militants. The paper also advocated the roundup and transfer to 'assembly centers or relocation camps' of at least 21 million 'American Negroes.' "[25]

The problem with this plan was that it was so blatantly anti-democratic that it alarmed even other factions within the reactionary Reagan White House, notably Attorney General William

French Smith, who "dispatched a letter to McFarlane August 2, 1984, lodging his objections and urging a delay in signing the directive."[26] The text of Smith's letter makes clear his concerns: "...I believe that the draft executive order raises serious substantive and public policy issues that should be further addressed before this proposal is submitted to the president. In short I believe that the role assigned to the Federal Emergency Management Agency (FEMA) on the revised executive order exceeds its proper function as a coordinating agency for emergency preparedness...This department and others have repeatedly raised serious policy and legal objections to the creation of an 'emergency czar' role for FEMA. Specific policy concerns regarding recent FEMA initiatives include the abandonment of the principle of 'several' agency responsibility and the expansion of the definition of severe emergencies to encompass 'routine' domestic law enforcement emergencies. Legal objections relate to the absence of presidential or congressional authorization for unilateral FEMA directives which seek to establish new federal government management structures or otherwise task cabinet departments and other federal agencies."[27]

Although it is not entirely clear how this inter-Administration dispute was resolved, "Congressional sources familiar with national disaster procedures said they believe Reagan did sign an executive order in 1984 that revised national military mobilization measures to deal with civilians in case of nuclear war or other crisis."[28] As a final legacy to the nation, just before leaving office, "Reagan signed Executive Order 12656 which assigned new emergency preparedness responsibilities. Reagan's final national security legacy to civil defense planning puts the NSC clearly in charge. In Section 104, EO 12656 states that the NSC is the principal forum for consideration of national security emergency preparedness policy and will arrange for executive branch liaison with, and assistance to, the congress and the federal judiciary on national security emergency preparedness matters."[29]

As well as can be determined, that is the story of how there came to exist a federal agency with the power to run roughshod over the U.S. Constitution in the event of any real or imagined "national emergency type situation," with no oversight from any other federal entity. Besides natural disasters, this could include widespread resistance to a foreign military intervention or the social unrest accompanying a massive economic depression. All of this could be largely irrelevant, however, as the Constitution of this country may well have become obsolete as far back as 1933, when President Roosevelt signed the War and Emergency Powers Act. As the U.S. Senate noted back in 1973:

"Since March the 9, 1933, the United States has been in a state of declared national emergency…This vast range of powers, taken together, confer enough authority to rule the country without reference to normal constitutional processes. Under the powers delegated by these statutes, the president may: seize property; organize and control the means of production; seize commodities; assign military forces abroad; institute martial law; seize and control all transportation and communication; regulate the operation of private enterprise; restrict travel; and, in a plethora of ways, control the lives of all American citizens."[30]

Section VII

The Benevolent
Superpower

CHAPTER 25

The Rogue Nation

The fact that some elements [of the U.S. government] may appear to be potentially "out of control" can be beneficial to creating and reinforcing fears and doubts within the minds of an adversary's decision makers...That the U.S. may become irrational and vindictive if its vital interests are attacked should be a part of the national persona we project to all adversaries...It hurts to portray ourselves as too fully rational and cool-headed...

— **U.S. Strategic Command "Essentials of Post-Cold War Deterrence," 1995 (U.S. Strategic Command, or STRATCOM, is the military entity responsible for formulating U.S. nuclear policy.)**

The White House appears to have taken the advice of STRATCOM to heart, as how else are we to explain the drive-by bombing of the Sudan in August of 1998? This action, taken against a sovereign nation with which the U.S. had no legitimate grievances, was a flagrant violation of international law that was harshly condemned, and rightly so, by the world community. The increasingly militarized approach to foreign policy, of which the Sudan bombing is but one recent example, is justified on the basis of fighting international "terrorism," which has largely replaced the old justification of fighting international communism. Of course, who is identified as a terrorist at any given time is largely determined by what best serves U.S. economic interests.

Yesterday's Abu Nidal morphs seamlessly into today's Osama bin Laden while Abdullah Ocalan takes the place of Yassir Arafat and Nelson Mandela. Both of the latter, not long ago vilified as "terrorist" leaders of "terrorist organizations," are now Nobel Peace Prize winners, widely praised in Washington and around the world. Other "terrorist" threats, such as Kaddafi in Libya and Assad in Syria, simply fade from view, with no explanation given as to why, though they remain in power, they no longer pose a threat to the sovereignty of the United States. Some groups formerly pegged as "terrorists," most recently the KLA (identified as such by the U.S. State Department in 1998), are suddenly reborn as "freedom fighters," again with no explanation offered as to how this miraculous transformation has taken place. Then there are those "terrorists" who suddenly become so only after years of serving as CIA "assets." Noriega of Panama, Aidid of Somalia, and the mother of all terrorists—Saddam Hussein—all fall into this category, all having been demonized only after ceasing to serve American interests. And of course there are the old standbys, such as the ever popular Fidel Castro, who can be trotted out at a moment's notice if no better villain is readily available.

All of these largely manufactured threats are used to justify an increasingly bloated level of military expenditures, euphemistically referred to as "defense spending," as well as a foreign policy increasingly reliant on naked aggression. In addition to the aerial bombardment and military occupation of Kosovo, the continued military presence in Bosnia, and the cruise missile attacks on the Sudan and Afghanistan, the United States continues to routinely launch air strikes against Iraq, though the American press has apparently decided that this is no longer news. All of these actions have been taken with virtually no debate in congress and an obvious contempt for public opinion. The overwhelming bipartisan support for vastly increasing the current military budget at every possible opportunity signals a continuation and escalation of U.S. belligerence.

The mainstream media have played a large part in creating a public tolerance for a greatly increased militarism by being a willing participant in this political shell game. American military actions are routinely glorified and sterilized, while the *terrorist du jour* is suitably vilified. Propaganda stories increasingly proliferate carrying preposterous warnings of near imminent nuclear attack on America from North Korea, Iraq, or some other allegedly "rogue" nation. By the Pentagon's logic, any nation not allied with the U.S. that is working on a nuclear weapons program is doing so for the express purpose of launching a preemptive strike against American soil.

Never is it suggested that these "rogue" nations, having witnessed the destructive power the United States was so eager to wield in such places as Iraq and Serbia, could feel a legitimate need to possess a meaningful deterrent against an international aggressor armed with some 6,000 long range nuclear missiles and a desire to appear "out of control." The notion that any nation would use such weaponry for offensive purposes, to launch a first strike at the United States, defies any rational analysis. Surely the cost to the aggressor nation of such an attack on America would be nothing less than the complete and total nuclear annihilation of the "rogue" nation and its people.

Of course, the State Department realizes that certain countries will not be deterred by this, because they are led by madmen who don't have the same respect for human life that we do. It would be foolhardy to expect these terrorist heads of state to act rationally. These men would willingly sacrifice their entire country for the chance to take out part of Manhattan. That is why we must always maintain our defenses against those who, in the words of one notorious rogue nation, "may become irrational and vindictive."

URGENT WARNING FROM THE NATIONAL INTELLIGENCE COUNCIL!

"The U.S. intelligence community warned Thursday that proliferation of medium-range ballistic missiles...presents an 'immediate, serious and growing threat' to U.S. forces and allies...Although the number of nuclear-armed missiles capable of striking the United States *has decreased since the Cold War*, the report says the world has grown less secure because missile technology has spread to unpredictable regimes such as North Korea and Iran...The report concludes that the United States will 'most likely' face ballistic missile threats over the next 15 years from Russia, China and North Korea, 'probably' from Iran and 'possibly' from Iraq."

Los Angeles Times, **September 10, 1999 (emphasis added)**

A ROGUE BY ANY OTHER NAME

"In November 1997, President Clinton issued a highly classified Presidential Decision Directive (PDD), giving new guidelines to the military on targeting nuclear weapons. According to reports, the new PDD allows for the use of nuclear weapons against 'rogue' states—those suspected of having access to weapons of mass destruction."

British American Security Information Council (BASIC)
Research Report 98.2, March 1998

"The U.S. nuclear arsenal is in the middle of a multi-billion dollar upgrade that will make it capable of quickly shifting between a greater number of limited contingencies all over the world...Additionally, new modifications of a number of U.S. nuclear weapons are currently underway in order to provide new capabilities suitable for targeting potential proliferators. In 1996, the B61-11 modification was identified by the Department of Defense as the 'weapon of choice' for targeting Libya's alleged underground chemical weapons plant at Tarhunah. Other weapons 'modifications' are in the pipeline."

British American Security Information Council (BASIC)
Research Report 98.2, March 1998

OOPS, SORRY

"The [Al Shifa] plant produced 50% of the pharmaceuticals available in the Sudan...It produced 90% of the antibiotics used for malaria which is the leading cause of death there...A single U.S. missile attack destroyed the single most important health facility in the Sudan and will cause thousands of deaths."

Ramsey Clark (former U.S. Attorney General),
Letter to the UN, November 1998

"The [Clinton] administration also blocked a proposed [UN] Security Council investigation into its bombing of Al-Shifa Pharmaceutical Plant in Khartoum. The investigation might have found that the United States lacked evidence to justify making the plant an appropriate military target."

Human Rights Watch "World Report 1999, Introduction"

WE'RE JUST A BENEVOLENT SUPERPOWER

"The United States spends more on arms annually, $275 billion presently, than the rest of the Security Council combined. U.S. arms expenditures are approximately 25 times the gross national product of Iraq. The U.S. has in its stockpiles more nuclear bombs, chemical and biological weapons, more aircraft, rockets and delivery systems in number and sophistication than the rest of the world combined. Included are twenty commissioned Trident II nuclear submarines any one of which could destroy Europe."

**Former U.S. Attorney General Ramsey Clark,
Letter to the UN, November 1998**

"Today, the United States spends more on military arms and other forms of 'national security' than the rest of the world combined. U.S. leaders preside over a global military apparatus of a magnitude never before seen in human history. In 1993 it included almost a half-million troops stationed at over 395 major military bases and hundreds of minor installations in thirty-five foreign countries, and a fleet larger in total tonnage and firepower than all the other navies of the world combined, consisting of missile cruisers, nuclear submarines, nuclear aircraft carriers, destroyers, and spy ships that sail every ocean and make port on every continent. U.S. bomber squadrons and long-range missiles can reach any target, carrying enough explosive force to destroy entire continents with an overkill capacity of more than 8,000 strategic nuclear weapons and 22,000 tactical ones."

Michael Parenti *Against Empire*, 1995

"[Nearly 70% of the military budget] is to provide men and weapons to fight in foreign countries in support of our allies and friends and for offensive operations in Third World countries... Another big chunk of the defense budget is the 20% allocated for our offensive nuclear force of bombers, missiles, and submarines whose job it is to carry nuclear weapons to the Soviet Union... Actual defense of the United States costs about 10% of the military budget and is the least expensive function performed by the Pentagon..."

Rear Admiral Gene LaRoque, United States Navy (retired), explaining the nature of the U.S. "defense" budget.

THE VOICES OF BELLIGERENCE

"Negotiations are a euphemism for capitulation if the shadow of power is not cast across the bargaining table"

Secretary of State George Schultz, April 1986

"If we have to use force, it is because we are America. We are the indispensable nation."

Secretary of State Madeleine Albright

"Another unacknowledged and unpleasant reality is that a more militant approach toward terrorism would, in virtually all cases, require us to *act violently and alone*."

Former CIA Director Robert M. Gates in the *New York Times*, August 16, 1998 (emphasis added)

"I will never apologize for the United States of America—I don't care what the facts are."

President George Bush, explaining his position on the downing of an Iranian commercial airliner. For the record, the facts were that the plane was on a routine flight in a commercial corridor in Iranian airspace, and the targeting of it by U.S forces was blatantly illegal.

COMING SOON TO A TOWN NEAR YOU—
URBAN WARFARE

"Inaugurated this week, Yodaville is the first urban bombing range for the U.S. military...The Marines hope their 'town' 35 miles southeast of Yuma will help the military develop more efficient and safer ways to attack villages, towns and cities from the air...Military experts predict that cities, where up to 70 percent of the world's population will live, will be the likely battlefields of the next century."

San Diego Union Tribune, June 18, 1999.

"For the future, mounted forces (tanks) must be ready to operate in urban settings...To meet the challenges that urban areas pose, the army must develop doctrine, training, organizations, materiel, and soldier-leaders. At Fort Knox, a facility is arising to fill these gaps. This new facility, a test bed for Force XXI, will integrate heavy weapons and mounted forces in urban operations...it will provide an unequaled opportunity for joint training across the spectrum of conventional and special forces...The site will be large and sophisticated. Plans include a 26-acre spread located on Fort Knox's northern training area...Its features will represent typical residential, municipal, and business districts found in cities."

Robert S. Cameron, Ph.D. "It Takes a Village To Prepare for Urban Combat...And Fort Knox Is Getting One," on the official Fort Knox website, which bills itself as the "Home of Mounted Warfare."

CHAPTER 26

Following the Blood Trail

[T]o maintain this position of disparity…we will have to dispense with all sentimentality and day-dreaming…We should cease to talk about vague and…unreal objectives such as human rights, the raising of the living standard, and democratization. The day is not far off when we are going to have to deal in straight power concepts…The less we are then hampered by idealistic slogans, the better.

— **U.S. State Department Policy Planning Study #23, 1948**

The hidden hand of the market will never work without a hidden fist—McDonald's cannot flourish without McDonnell Douglas, the designer of the F-15.

— **Thomas L. Friedman "A Manifesto for the Fast World," New York Times Magazine, March 28, 1999**

The nationalist not only does not disapprove of atrocities committed by his own side, but he has a remarkable capacity for not even hearing about them.

— **George Orwell, author of 1984 (1903–1950)**

Since World War II, American military actions, in one form or another, have caused more death and destruction around the world than have the actions of any other country. Some of these interventions have been conducted overtly, with large scale deployment of U.S. troops, while others have involved the covert use of American troops and air power. Still others have involved proxy armies armed, trained, funded and directed by the U.S. Central Intelligence Agency. Almost all of these slaughters have been directed at people of color, particularly in Southeast Asia and Central America. The most egregious of these crimes against humanity are summarized here. These are the unseen and unheard victims of the relentless drive by the United States' corporate and military elite for global economic domination; they have given their lives so that we in America may prosper.

Korea

Year: 1951–1953

Estimated Deaths*: 1,000,000–2,000,00

Overview: Massive aerial bombardment and "scorched earth" policy on the ground led to wholesale slaughter of civilians and virtually complete destruction of civilian infrastructure. Also featured extensive use of napalm and frequent threats of nuclear strikes.

Bonus Points: Featured credible allegations, including the confessions of some of the U.S. pilots who had flown the missions, of the extensive use of germ warfare using bio-warfare agents acquired from German and Japanese fascists. The pilots were said to be brainwashed.

Vietnam

Year: 1960–1975

Estimated Deaths*: 1,000,000–2,000,000

Overview: Eerily similar to the Korean intervention, though of longer duration. Featured years of relentless aerial bombardment with cluster bombs, conventional bombs, napalm, agent orange, white phosphorous explosives, as well as repeated threats of a nuclear strike.

Bonus Points: Featured credible allegations, including a recent acknowledgment by a member of the Joint Chiefs of Staff, of the use of Sarin nerve gas on numerous occasions, including its use against U.S. servicemen who had deserted the war.

Guatemala

Year: 1962–1980s

Estimated Deaths*: 200,000

Overview: In one of the most well-documented cases of CIA complicity in state-sponsored slaughter, the United States trained, armed, and funded the military apparatus of our client state for years while it engaged in the wholesale torture and killing of tens of thousands of its people.

Bonus Points: The vast majority of those killed by the U.S.-backed Guatemalan government were Mayan Indians, thereby paying tribute to that time-honored American tradition of conducting acts of genocide against indigenous peoples.

Laos

Year: 1964–1973

Estimated Deaths*: 500,000+

Overview: Not content with the level of destruction in Vietnam, covert carpet bombing of Laos began, eventually dumping some 750,000 tons of bombs on the country. The Plain of Jars, frequently described as one of the most naturally beautiful places on earth, was hit repeatedly with cluster bomb attacks.

Bonus Points: More than a quarter of a century after the bombs stopped falling, unexploded cluster bomblets littering the country-side continue to this day to kill and maim hundreds of Laotian civilians. Meanwhile, the U.S steadfastly refuses to assist in any clean up efforts.

Indonesia

Year: 1965

Estimated Deaths*: 500,000–1,000,000

Overview: Following a CIA-backed military coup, a bloodbath ensued that claimed up to a million lives. Lists of suspected communists and communist sympathizers were supplied to the Indonesian military by the U.S. to facilitate the barbarism.

Bonus Points: Indonesia's military and domestic police forces continue to this day to be one of the United States' best customers for weapons, training, and torture devices.

Cambodia

Year: 1969–1975

Estimated Deaths*: 1,000,000–2,000,000

Overview: Still not content with the destruction being wrought upon Southeast Asia, the U.S. began a massive covert bombing campaign against Cambodia, resulting in famine, economic chaos, and a staggeringly high death toll.

Bonus Points: The desperate conditions created by the bombing set the stage for the rise to power of the Khmer Rouge, resulting in yet another round of death and destruction for the besieged country. (Death toll above is the total of the two factors.)

Indonesia

Year. 1975

Estimated Deaths*: 200,000

Overview: Not content with the recent mass murder of its own citizens, the U.S.-backed government of Indonesia invaded East Timor just one day after a visit by President Gerald Ford and Henry Kissinger. As many as a third of the tiny island's people were exterminated using American supplied weaponry.

Bonus Points: The Indonesian government, still kept propped up with U.S. taxpayers' money, continues to this day to be one of the worst human rights abusers on the planet.

El Salvador

Year: 1980–1994

Estimated Deaths*: 75,000+

Overview: Massive amounts of arms, training, and funding were poured into El Salvador to prop up the puppet government against a popular uprising. Featured the covert use of U.S. air power and ground forces, as well as the training, at the "School of the Americas," of the leaders of the right-wing death squads which executed thousands of Salvadorans.

Bonus Points: Some of the highlights of the death squad activities included the assassination of Archbishop Oscar Romero, the execution of six Jesuit priests along with their housekeeper and her daughter, the rape and execution of four American church women, and the mass execution of some 800 civilians at the village of El Mozote.

Nicaragua

Year: 1981–1990

Estimated Deaths*: tens of thousands

Overview: Following the fall of the Somoza regime, which had been backed for decades by the U.S., the CIA formed and armed the covert army known as the "Contras" from the remains of Somoza's National Guard. Assisted by covert U.S. air power, this proxy army inflicted considerable death and destruction across the Nicaraguan countryside.

Bonus Points: An overwhelming body of evidence exists indicating that the Contra war caused considerable destruction within the "inner cities" (i.e. black neighborhoods) of America as well, as cheap cocaine was marketed to fund the war effort.

Iraq

Year: 1990–?

Estimated Deaths*: 1,500,000+

Overview: A six-week aerial bombardment directed at the civilian infrastructure featured the use of fuel-air bombs, depleted uranium, napalm, cluster bombs, cruise missiles, and "smart bombs." Followed by nearly a decade of exceedingly harsh economic sanctions and periodic bombings.

Bonus Points: Featured extensive use of radioactive DU weaponry, which has resulted in alarmingly high cancer rates and birth abnormalities. Also established a new framework for how wars would be covered by the press.

Yugoslavia

Year: 1999–?

Estimated Deaths: ????

Overview: Like Iraq, a sustained bombing campaign directed against the civilian infrastructure, though of longer duration. Followed by a deployment of "peacekeeping forces." The length of the engagement and the extent of the carnage remain to be seen.

Bonus Points: So cynical and contemptuous of public opinion have Washington's war planners become that virtually no effort was made to "sell" this war to the American people in advance of the commencement of bombing, thereby providing a "sell as you go" model for future military engagements.

"I spent 33 years in the Marines. Most of my time being a high-class muscle man for Big business, for Wall Street and the bankers. In short, I was a racketeer for capitalism. I helped purify Nicaragua for the international banking house of Brown Brothers in 1909–1912. I helped make Mexico and especially Tampico safe for American oil interests in 1914. I brought light to the Dominican Republic for American sugar interests in 1916. I helped make Haiti and Cuba a decent place for the National City Bank boys to collect

174

revenue in. I helped in the rape of half a dozen Central American republics for the benefit of Wall Street."

U.S. Marine Corps Major General Smedley Darlington Butler**,
in *Common Sense*, November 1935

"I believe that if we had and would keep our dirty, bloody, dollar soaked fingers out of the business of these [Third World] nations so full of depressed, exploited people, they will arrive at a solution of their own...And if unfortunately their revolution must be of the violent type because the 'haves' refuse to share with the 'have-nots' by any peaceful method, at least what they get will be their own, and not the American style, which they don't want and above all don't want crammed down their throats by Americans."

General David Sharp, former United States Marine Commandant, 1966

"The greatest crime since World War II has been U.S. foreign policy."

Ramsey Clark, former U.S. Attorney General
under President Lyndon Johnson

"We're going to become guilty, in my judgement, of being the greatest threat to the peace of the world. It's an ugly reality, and we Americans don't like to face up to it. I hate to think of the chapter of American history that's going to be written in the future in connection with our outlawry in Southeast Asia."

Senator Wayne Morse (D-OR), 1967

*Estimating the death toll from any military engagement is always problematic. One of many factors complicating this task is the desire of the respective governments to deliberately misrepresent the body count. The country perpetrating the slaughter seeks to downplay the carnage so as to avoid the revulsion of its people and the world community. The nation unfortunate enough to be the victim of aggression frequently downplays the actual number of casualties as well, due to a sense of national pride and a desire not to panic its own citizenry. The figures given here are based on the best available evidence from a variety of sources, including

William Blum's Killing Hope; U.S. Military and CIA Interventions Since World War II, *Howard Zinn's* A People's History of the United States, *and* A Century Of U.S. Military Interventions: From Wounded Knee to Yugoslavia, *compiled by Zoltan Grossman.*

**General Butler, though unknown to most Americans today, is one of the true unsung heroes of American history. In 1933, General Butler virtually single-handedly foiled a coup d'etat, well-financed by a cabal of very prominent and wealthy U.S. industrialists, that would have established an overtly fascist military dictatorship in the United States. Though this was officially denied by the Congressional McCormack-Dickstein Committee's public report, and quickly forgotten, the committee's internal summation to the House of Representatives tells a considerably different story: "In the last few weeks of the committee's life it received evidence showing that certain persons had made an attempt to establish a fascist organization in this country...There is no question that these attempts were discussed, were planned, and might have been placed in execution when and if the financial backers deemed it expedient...[coup conspirator Gerald] MacGuire denied [General Butler's] allegations under oath, but your committee was able to verify all the pertinent statements made to General Butler, with the exception of the direct statement suggesting the creation of the organization. This, however, was corroborated in the correspondence of MacGuire with his principal, Robert Sterling Clark, of New York City, while MacGuire was abroad studying the various forms of veterans' organizations of fascist character." From John L. Spivak, A Man in His Time.

CHAPTER 27

Low-Intensity Genocide

Lesley Stahl: *"We have heard that half a million children have died. That is more than died in Hiroshima. And, you know, is the price worth it?"*

Secretary of State Madeleine Albright: *"I think this is a very hard choice. But the price—we think the price is worth it."*

— **An exchange on CBS's** *60 Minutes,* **May 1996**

The U.S. media have become quite adept at sterilizing war, shamelessly blurring the line between war and entertainment. The cable news networks in particular have pioneered the presentation of armed conflict as part video game and part miniseries, complete with theme music and logos. In a video game war, there are no apparent casualties. And when a country with the world's premier military force attacks an essentially defenseless enemy from the air, only the "bad guys" die anyway. Their corpses are hardly worth taking the time to count.

THESE SANCTIONS REALLY SEEM TO BE WORKING

"The six-week war in 1991 resulted in the large-scale destruction of military and civilian infrastructures alike...The sanctions imposed on Iraq and related circumstances have prevented the country from repairing all of its damaged or destroyed infrastructure, and whenever attempts have been made, these have been incomplete. This applies to electricity generating and water purification plants, sewage treatment facilities and communication and transportation networks. This has affected the quality of life of countless Iraqi citizens...The vast majority of the country's population has been on a semi-starvation diet for years. This tragic situation has tremendous implications on the health status of the population and on their quality of life, not only for the present generation, but for the future generation as well...The reduction in the import of medicines, owing to a lack of financial resources, as well as a lack of minimum health care facilities, insecticides, pharmaceutical and other related equipment and appliances, have crippled the health care services, which in pre-war years were of a high quality. Assessment reports rightly remarked that the quality of health care in Iraq, due to the six-week 1991 war and the subsequent sanctions imposed on the country, has been literally put back by at least 50 years. Diseases such as malaria, typhoid and cholera, which were once almost under control, have rebounded since 1991 at epidemic levels, with the health sector as a helpless witness...Very rarely has the impact of sanctions on millions of people been documented. Severe economic hardship, a semi-starvation diet, high levels of disease, scarcity of essential drugs and, above all, the psycho-social trauma and anguish of a bleak future, have led to numerous families being broken up leading to distortions in social norms...The impact of this unfortunate situation on the infant and child population in particular in Iraq needs special attention. It is not only the data on morbidity and mortality that tell the story, but equally important are the crippling effects of many of these morbidities which are often forgotten. The psychological trauma of the six-week 1991 war and the terrible hardships enduring with the sanctions since then can be expected to leave indelible marks on the mental health and behavioural patterns of these children when they grow to adulthood. This tragic aspect of the impact of the war and conditions surrounding the sanctions is rarely articulated, but the world community should seriously consider the implications of an entire generation of children growing up with such traumatized mental handicaps, if of course, they survive at all."

The World Health Organization "Health Conditions of the Population in Iraq Since the Gulf Crisis," March 1996

"The Contracting Parties confirm that genocide, whether committed in time of peace or in time of war, is a crime under international law which they undertake to prevent and to punish. In the present Convention, genocide means any of the following acts committed with intent to destroy, in whole or in part, a national, ethnical, racial, or religious group, as such:...(c) Deliberately inflicting on the group conditions of life calculated to bring about its physical destruction in whole or in part...Persons committing genocide or any of the acts enumerated in Article III shall be punished, whether they are constitutionally responsible rulers, public officials, or private individuals."

United Nations Convention on the Prevention and Punishment of the Crime of Genocide, 1948

WHAT WILL HENRY HYDE TELL THESE CHILDREN?

"Sanctions have taken the lives of well over one million persons, 60% of whom are children under five years of age. The 1991 bombing campaign destroyed electric, water and sewage plants, as well as agricultural, food and medical production facilities. All of these structures continue to be inoperative, or function at sub-minimal levels, because the sanctions have made it impossible to buy spare parts for their repair. This bombing campaign, together with the total embargo in place since August 1990 was, and is, an attack against the civilian population of Iraq."

"U.S. Bishops' Statement on Iraq," January 1998 (Signed by 53 Catholic bishops.)

"4,500 children under the age of 5 are dying each month from hunger and disease...Many are living on the very margin of survival."

UNICEF, October 1996

"More than one million Iraqis have died—567,000 of them children—as a direct consequence of economic sanctions...As many as 12 percent of the children surveyed in Baghdad are wasted, 28 percent stunted and 29 percent underweight."

United Nation's Food and Agriculture Organization (FAO), December 1995

"The Cuban and Iraqi instances make it abundantly clear that economic sanctions are, at their core, a war against public health. Our professional ethic demands the defense of public health. Thus, as physicians, we have a moral imperative to call for the end of sanctions. Having found the cause, we must act to remove it. Continuing to allow our reason to sleep will produce more monsters."

New England Journal of Medicine, **Editorial, April 24, 1997**

"The increase in mortality reported in public hospitals for children under five years of age (an excess of some 40,000 deaths yearly compared with 1989) is mainly due to diarrhea, pneumonia and malnutrition. In those over five years of age, the increase (an excess of some 50,000 deaths yearly compared with 1989) is associated with heart disease, hypertension, diabetes, cancer, liver or kidney diseases... With the substantial increase in mortality, under-registration of deaths is a growing problem...the GDP per capita has [been] reduced from $3500 to $600 and the current salary of public workers now averages about $3 to $5 per month...Historically, Iraq has given education a high priority. However, the protracted economic hardship on Iraqi population has seriously affected every level of formal and informal education."

UNICEF "Situation Analysis of Children and Women in Iraq," April 1998

"[Iraq] has experienced a shift from relative affluence to massive poverty. In marked contrast to the prevailing situation prior to the events of 1990–91, the infant mortality rates in Iraq today are among the highest in the world, low infant birth weight affects at least 23% of all births, chronic malnutrition affects every fourth child under five years of age, only 41% of the population have regular access to clean water, 83% of all schools need substantial repairs. The ICRC states that the Iraqi health-care system is today in a decrepit state. UNDP calculates that it would take 7 billion U.S. dollars to rehabilitate the power sector country-wide."

United Nations Report on the Current Humanitarian Situation in Iraq, March 1999

On January 18, 1999, the Iraqi Minister of Health, Oumid Medhat Mubarak, put the total number of Iraqi deaths due to the combined effects of the initial war, the repeated military strikes and the prolonged sanctions at 1,873,464.

I'LL TAKE THAT BET

"I am willing to make a bet to anyone here that we care more about the Iraqi people than Saddam Hussein does."

Secretary of State Madeleine Albright, February 1998

HOW ABOUT WHEN HELL FREEZES OVER

"We are not interested in seeing a relaxation of sanctions as long as Saddam Hussein is in power."

Secretary of State James Baker, May 1991

"There is no difference between my policy and the policy of the (Bush) Administration...I have no intention of normalizing relations with him."

President-Elect Bill Clinton, January 1993

"We do not agree with the nations who argue that if Iraq complies with its obligations concerning weapons of mass destruction, sanctions should be lifted. Our view, which is unshakable, is that Iraq must prove its peaceful intentions...And the evidence is overwhelming that Saddam Hussein's intentions will never be peaceful."

Secretary of State Madeleine Albright, March 1997

"Sanctions may stay on in perpetuity."

U.S. Ambassador Bill Richardson, August 1997

U.S. COMBAT CASUALTIES *

- 55 killed
- 155 wounded
- 30 missing
- 9 prisoners of war

*Includes 28 killed, 100 injured in Scud attack on Dhahran.

IRAQI LOSSES

- 2,085 tanks
- 962 armored vehicles
- 1,005 artillery pieces
- 103 aircraft destroyed; 139 in Iran.

Washington Post chart showing that while selfless Americans sacrificed life and limb in Operation Desert Storm, Iraqis lost only military equipment.

"What he has just done is to ensure that the sanctions will be there until the end of time…"

President Bill Clinton, November 1997

DOES THIS MEAN WE HAVE TO BOMB OURSELVES?

The United States, as a signatory to various international treaties banning the testing, manufacture and development of chemical and biological weapons, *is required by law* to open its weapons facilities to UN inspectors to verify treaty compliance. In defiance of the treaties' provisions, the United States Senate passed a bill in 1997 allowing the president to deny international inspections of U.S. weapons facilities "on grounds of national security."

Associated Press, February 27, 1998

CHAPTER 28

Post-Modern Chemical Warfare

They call it "The Night of the Witches," those horrible hours that began at precisely 1 a.m. April 18, when NATO bombs and missiles rained in force on this Serbian city [Pancevo]. Within seconds, they demolished a refinery, a fertilizer plant and an American-built petrochemical complex that released a toxic cloud so dense and potentially lethal that its effects can be felt here even today—and will be, perhaps, for decades.

— ***Los Angeles Times*** **"Yugoslav City Battling Toxic Enemies," July 6, 1999**

Come back, my friend, in 10 years. Then you will find half the people of Pancevo are dead, just like the fish.

— **Local fisherman Dragomir Djuric, in the** ***Chicago Tribune***, **July 8, 1999**

The United States has become quite adept in recent years at waging what can best be described as indirect chemical warfare. This is accomplished by using conventional bombs to disburse chemical agents already known to be on the ground. The technique, perfected in "Operation Desert Storm," was used quite extensively in the assault on Yugoslavia. This master stroke of military strategy allows the United States to reap the military "benefits" of waging chemical warfare, while largely escaping the international condemnation for having done so. The city of Pancevo became just one of many chemical warfare testing grounds.

WE MIGHT HAVE ACCIDENTALLY HIT IT ONCE

"The petrochemical and fertilizer complex that dominated the economy of this city of 120,000 is now virtually reduced to rubble by the NATO strikes. Warplanes rained missiles and bombs on Pancevo for nearly three months, from March 24 to the last raid June 8. The raids blew up storage tanks and released thousands of tons of toxic chemicals into the environment. Pancevo was enveloped in a noxious cloud of smoke and fumes for days."

Chicago Tribune "Serbs Allege NATO Raids Caused Toxic Catastrophe," July 8, 1999

"According to the log he (Professor Mico Martinovic) maintained, NATO bombed the chemical complex at Pancevo on 23 days, hitting it with at least 56 bombs or missiles."

Chicago Tribune "Serbs Allege NATO Raids Caused Toxic Catastrophe," July 8, 1999

"On the night of April 18…NATO bombers scored direct hits on facilities holding 1,500 tons of vinyl-chloride monomer, 250 tons of chlorine, 1,800 tons of ethylene dichloride and 15,000 tons of ammonia."

Chicago Tribune "Serbs Allege NATO Raids Caused Toxic Catastrophe," July 8, 1999

HOW WERE WE SUPPOSED TO KNOW
WHAT WAS THERE?

"Mayor Mikovic produced municipal records documenting that the petrochemical plant that opened in 1978 was built by three American companies and a German firm. Two other U.S.

corporations, along with a French concern, built the oil refinery. And the fertilizer plant was a joint venture by the U.S., Spain and the Netherlands."

Los Angeles Times "Yugoslav City Battling
Toxic Enemies," July 6, 1999

WE'VE BEEN INFORMED THAT
THE DAMAGE WAS MINIMAL

"VCM's [vinyl chloride monomers] have reached concentrations of 10,600 times more than permitted levels near the Pancevo petrochemical plant. Polluted clouds carried the products of combusted VCM's: phosgene, chlorine, chlorine oxides and nitrogen oxides."

**The Regional Environmental Center for Central and Eastern Europe
"Assessment of the Environmental Impact of Military Activities
During the Yugoslavia Conflict," June 1999**

"Physicians in [Pancevo]...have privately recommended that all women who were in town that night avoid pregnancy for at least the next two years."

Los Angeles Times "Yugoslav City Battling
Toxic Enemies," July 6, 1999

"Following the Pancevo incidents, a cloud of smoke some 15 kilometres in length lasted for ten days."

**The Regional Environmental Center for Central and Eastern Europe
"Assessment of the Environmental Impact of Military Activities
During the Yugoslavia Conflict," June 1999**

"[T]he ground in and around Pancevo is saturated with ammonia, mercury, naptha, acids, dioxins and other toxins that leaked and burned out of the factories that night..."

Los Angeles Times "Yugoslav City Battling
Toxic Enemies," July 6, 1999

"Specific impacts include the following: PCB's have been released from damaged transformer stations....Oil products have leaked into the Danube River from the Pancevo industrial center...More than one hundred tonnes of ammonia leaked into the Danube...More than one thousand tonnes of ethylene dichloride spilled from the Pancevo petrochemical complex into the Danube...Over a thousand tonnes of natrium hydroxide were spilled from Pancevo into the Danube River...Heavy metals: copper, cadmium, chromium and lead, at rates double the maximum allowed concentration, have been registered in Romania's Danube."

The Regional Environmental Center for Central and Eastern Europe
"Assessment of the Environmental Impact of Military Activities
During the Yugoslavia Conflict," June 1999

"Several of the above-described toxic compounds released after bombing can cause chronic health problems. Perhaps the most dangerous is depleted uranium, but there are also other carcinogenic and toxic substances, such as vinyl chloride monomers, which have been released. Many of the compounds released can cause miscarriages and birth defects. Others are associated with fatal nerve and liver diseases."

The Regional Environmental Center for Central and Eastern Europe
"Assessment of the Environmental Impact of Military Activities
During the Yugoslavia Conflict," June 1999

"People exposed to the cloud have already started dying. Children with chemical-singed lungs find it painful to breathe and an unusual number of women suffered miscarriages following the bombing."

Earth Island Journal, **Winter 1999–2000**

THE CIA GAVE US LOUSY MAPS

"Although perhaps the most dramatic, Pancevo is one of many environmental disasters that are legacies of NATO's war on Yugoslavia and its dominant republic, Serbia—78 days of aerial assaults on power plants, factories, fuel refineries and storage tanks."

Los Angeles Times **"Yugoslav City Battling**
Toxic Enemies," July 6, 1999

WE FEEL THE PROBLEM HAS BEEN CONTAINED

"The WWF (World Wide Fund for Nature) found evidence that toxic pollutants released close to places hit by the NATO bombing were now spreading into surrounding areas."

BBC News "Danube Pollution Warning," September 14, 1999

"In an interview with the BBC, Yugoslavian hydrogeologist Momir Komatina worried that the region's underground water resources—which serve about 90 percent of Serbia's domestic and industrial needs—are now at risk. He noted that the imperiled water tables extend well beyond Serbia and into southern Europe."

Earth Island Journal, **Winter 1999–2000**

WE SPECIFICALLY TOLD THEM
NOT TO EAT THE BROWN ACID

"Stories are circulating of outsized fruits and vegetables, of trees turning bright yellow in midsummer."

Chicago Tribune **"Serbs Allege NATO Raids Caused Toxic Catastrophe," July 8, 1999**

IT TURNS OUT IT WAS ALL
JUST SERB PROPAGANDA

"After reports of American jungle defoliation and attempts at weather manipulation during the Vietnam War, the international community adopted the first specific rules of war—two additions to the Geneva Convention and a separate treaty—that tell combatants not to target the environment, [Air Force Lt. Col. Michael] Schmitt said."

San Jose Mercury News **"UN to Probe Claims of Harm to Environment," May 16, 1999**

"A NATO official…reiterated NATO's position that it tries not to damage the environment in its bombings and knows of no specific bombing-caused problems."

San Jose Mercury News **"UN to Probe Claims of Harm to Environment," May 16, 1999**

CHAPTER 29

Little Nukes

*The Committee concludes that it is unlikely that health
effects reports by Gulf War Veterans today are the result of
exposure to depleted uranium during the Gulf War.*

— **Presidential Advisory Committee of Gulf War Veterans'
Illnesses "Final Report," December 1996**

Beginning in the Gulf War, U.S. military forces began using a
new type of weapon whose attributes are rarely discussed in
the American press. These are sometimes referred to
euphemistically as "tank killers" or "anti-tank rounds," though
what it is that renders them so effective for this purpose is never
mentioned. These rounds are credited with destroying some 1,400
Iraqi tanks, performing well above Pentagon expectations and
thereby assuring their continued use in future U.S. wars of aggression, as their deployment in both Bosnia and Kosovo clearly
demonstrates.

Composed of an extremely dense metal, these weapons are able
to concentrate an enormous amount of weight at the point of
impact, giving them unprecedented penetrating power. As an added
bonus, the material from which these tank killers are manufactured
is pyrophoric, fragmenting and igniting upon impact. And best of
all, the material is cheap and readily available. In fact, prior to its
recently discovered military use, vast stockpiles of it sat unused for
years, decades even. Of course, in those days it had a different name
than it does today. Back then we knew it simply as "nuclear waste."

Today, the military knows it as DU, or depleted uranium. It is, in fact, a radioactive byproduct of the nuclear weapons and power industries, which previously had presented these industries with long-term storage problems.

But not any more. Thanks to the ingenuity of U.S. weapons designers, we are now able to dump our radioactive waste on "rogue" nations such as Serbia and Iraq. In "Operation Desert Storm" alone, some 940,000 small-caliber DU rounds were fired into Iraq and Kuwait from such aircraft as the A10 Warthog and the Apache helicopter. In addition, anywhere from 6,000 to 14,000 large-caliber DU rounds were fired from U.S. tanks. All told, anywhere from 40 to 300 tons of radioactive uranium were left littering the battlefields of the Gulf war, several times the 25 tons that a report by Britain's Atomic Energy Authority concluded could cause "500,000 potential deaths."

Thus we see that, as the true believers have always said, the ingenuity of American capitalists has triumphed over one of the most troublesome of environmental problems—nuclear waste disposal. At the same time, the U.S. military has gained yet another weapon which has the ability to continue killing long after the war in which it was deployed has ended. The Pentagon has long shown a certain fondness for such weapons, particularly the ever-popular cluster bombs that have had a starring role in every military engagement from Vietnam to Kosovo. DU will likely play an increasingly prominent role in future U.S. interventions, of which there are sure to be many. With 500,000 tons of raw material readily available, it's not likely that supplies will be diminished any time soon. This should provide America's architects of war with plenty of ammunition with which to perfect the technique of quietly waging low-grade nuclear war—one bullet at a time.

ALL IS FAIR IN LOVE AND WAR

"If DU enters the body, it has the potential to generate significant medical consequences. The risks associated with DU in the body are both chemical and radiological...Personnel inside or near vehicles struck by DU penetrators could receive significant internal exposures."

Army Environmental Policy Institute (AEPI) "Health and Environmental Consequences of Depleted Uranium Use in the U.S. Army," June 1995

"Inhaled insoluble oxides stay in the lungs longer and pose a potential cancer risk due to radiation. Ingested DU dust can also pose both a radioactive and a toxicity risk."

United States General Accounting Office "Operation Desert Storm: Army Not Adequately Prepared to Deal With Depleted Uranium Contamination," January 1993 (GAO/NSIAD-93-90)

"DU is inherently toxic. This toxicity can be managed, but it cannot be changed…"

Army Environmental Policy Institute (AEPI) "Health and Environmental Consequences of Depleted Uranium Use in the U.S. Army," June 1995

"Short-term effects of high doses can result in death, while long-term effects of low doses have been implicated in cancer."

AMMCOM "Kinetic Energy Penetrator Long Term Strategy Study," Appendix D, Danesi, July 1990

"[The Pentagon's] assertion that no Gulf War veterans could be ill from exposure to DU…contradicts numerous pre- and post-war reports, some from the U.S. Army itself."

Senator Russell Feingold (D-WI), September 1998

IN UNRELATED NEWS

"[T]he number of cancer cases and birth defects among Iraqi civilians in Basra, Al-Amarah, An-Nasiriyah and Ad-Diwaniyah has grown at least threefold since the 1991 Persian Gulf War, according to Iraqi doctors and medical records. Knight Ridder has obtained unpublished Iraqi government documents that show a sharp postwar rise in cancer rates in southern Iraq…Most alarming, doctors say, is a sharp rise in leukemia cases among children, including some who were born more than nine months after the end of the war, suggesting that some environmental carcinogens may have lingered long after the war ended or that some war-related contaminants may be causing genetic damage."

San Jose Mercury News, March 19, 1998

"The journalist and author Robert Fisk last night said 'an explosion of child cancers in southern Iraq appeared to be intimately linked to weapons used by U.S.-led forces in the Gulf War...Mr. Fisk spoke of recent visits to Iraq and uncovering evidence of an unusually high incidence of cancer there since the Gulf War, particularly in the south. In Basra, where the last tank battles of the war had been fought, people were reporting 'football sized tomatoes, carrots of a strange purple color, water that no longer tasted normal.'"

Irish Times, "Iraqi Child Cancers Link to Gulf
War Weapons," November 30, 1999

"Two leading authorities on the effects of depleted uranium (DU) have ... said DU weapons should be banned, because their use was a crime against humanity. It contaminated the environment, and caused suffering to civilians. Professor Sharma [professor emeritus of chemistry, University of Waterloo, Ontario] ... told BBC News Online: 'Based on the samples I have examined, I think between 5% and 12% of those who were exposed to DU may expect to die of cancer.'"

BBC News, "Depleted Uranium Ban Demanded," December 17, 1999

"A British biologist, Roger Coghill, says he expects the depleted uranium (DU) weapons used by U.S. aircraft over Kosovo will cause more than 10,000 fatal cancer cases ... In mid-June scientists at Kozani in northern Greece were reporting that radiation levels were 25% above normal whenever the wind blew from the direction of Kosovo. And Bulgarian researchers reported finding levels eight times higher than usual within Bulgaria itself, and up to 30 times higher in Yugoslavia."

**BBC News, "Depleted Uranium 'Threatens Balkan
Cancer Epidemic,'" July 30, 1999**

For further information on DU, see:

Helen Caldicott, Michio Kaku, Jay Gould, and Ramsey Clark "Metal of Dishonor: How Depleted Uranium Penetrates Steel, Radiates People and Contaminates the Environment."

CHAPTER 30

Space Cowboys

The technological research is already under way to convert the Strategic Defense Initiative, the "Star Wars" anti-missile program, from a supposedly defensive system into a web of expensive, Earth-circling offensive weapons...SDI, the proper name for "Star Wars," officially stands for the Strategic Defense Initiative. But it has secretly become the Space Domination Initiative.

— **San Jose Mercury News, August 2, 1992**

Historically, military forces have evolved to protect national interests and investments—both military and economic... During the early portion of the 21st Century, space power will also evolve into a separate and equal medium of warfare.

— **U.S. Space Command "Vision for 2020," 1998 (U.S. Space Command was created by the Pentagon to coordinate the efforts of the Army, Navy and Air Force to "institutionalize the use of space.")**

Suppose someone were to tell you that hidden beneath the stated agenda of the so-called "Star Wars" missile defense system—originally proposed by the Reagan Administration under the official title of "Strategic Defense Initiative," and now known under Clinton as the "Ballistic Missile Defense" system—there existed a program that had nothing to do with missile defense. Suppose they were to tell you that what was being developed was a space-based *offensive* weapons system that would enable the United States to solidify its absolute military superiority by controlling space. Suppose further that they were to tell you that this system will involve space-based super lasers capable of destroying targets on land and at sea, and that these lasers will be powered by nuclear reactors that will likewise be deployed in space. Suppose they were to go on to tell you that tens of billions of dollars have already been spent on the program and that some elements of the system are already in place. You would naturally assume that this person did not have a firm grasp on reality. Unless, of course, it happened that the person relaying this information to you was one of the officials in charge of the project.

AND SOME PEOPLE DON'T WANT TO REPORT IT, EITHER

"Some people don't want to hear this, and it sure isn't in vogue, but—absolutely—we're going to fight in space. We're going to fight from space and we're going to fight into space...We will engage terrestrial targets someday—ships, airplanes, land targets—from space."

Commander-in-Chief of U.S. Space Command, Joseph W. Ashy, in *Aviation Week and Space Technology*, **August 9, 1996**

"A good place to comprehend how the United States plans to fight 21st century wars is beneath a mountain in Colorado. A 1,400-foot tunnel bored through Cheyenne Mountain leads to an underground village of spring-mounted buildings, built to sway in a nuclear attack. These headquarters of the North American Aerospace Defense Command are webbed to the nearby Falcon Air Force Base, the first operational center for 'Star Wars.' Their combined computers, crunching data from radar installations, ground-based telescopes and satellites 22,300 miles above Earth, offer a real-time view of all missile launches and bomber runs around the world, and everything orbiting the planet, down to space junk the size of a softball....The Pentagon wants the next war to be controlled and all but decided with weapons in the 'high ground' of space, directed from electronic control rooms in places like Cheyenne Mountain."

San Jose Mercury News, **August 2, 1992**

SO DON'T EVEN THINK ABOUT PISSING US OFF

"With regard to space dominance, we have it, we like it and we're going to keep it."

Keith Hall, Assistant Secretary of the Air Force for Space, speaking to the National Space Club, 1997

"[T]he confidence that we can police the world without retaliation was reflected earlier in the year in a leaked Bush administration defense planning document for 1994–1999."

San Jose Mercury News, **August 2, 1992**

COOL! CAN I ENTER MY INITIALS IF I GET THE MOST KILLS?

"In the next two decades, new technologies will allow the fielding of space-based weapons of devastating effectiveness to be used to deliver energy and mass as force projection in tactical and strategic conflict...These advances will enable lasers with reasonable mass and cost to effect very many kills."

United States Air Force "New World Vistas: Air and Space Power for the 21st Century," 1996

"A space blockade would effectively ring the planet with barbed wire, making the whole world our security zone. Errant countries would be punished from the sky, with American troops entering the fray only to conduct mop-up operations."

San Jose Mercury News, **August 2, 1992**

WE'RE GOING TO NEED A REALLY LONG EXTENSION CORD

"[P]ower limitations impose restrictions…a natural technology to enable high power is nuclear power in space. Setting the emotional issues of nuclear power aside, this technology offers a viable alternative for large amounts of power in space."

United States Air Force "New World Vistas: Air and Space Power for the 21st Century," 1996

AT LEAST IT'S ALL FOR A GOOD CAUSE

"U.S. Space Command—dominating the space dimension of military operations *to protect U.S. interests and investment.* Integrating Space Forces into war-fighting capabilities across the full spectrum of conflict."

U.S. Space Command "Vision for 2020," 1998 (emphasis added)

Much of the material in this chapter was derived from the work of Professor Karl Grossman of the State University of New York, the premier researcher and writer on this and related subjects. Mr. Grossman is the author of *The Wrong Stuff: The Space Program's Nuclear Threat To Our Planet.*

CHAPTER 31

How's the Weather Up There?

If human equality is to be forever averted—if the High, as we have called them, are to keep their places permanently— then the prevailing mental condition must be controlled insanity.

— George Orwell 1984

The less one is aware of the invisible war, the more receptive one is to its ongoing process of demoralization, for the insensate human is vulnerable, malleable, weak, and ripe for control.

— Anton Szandor LaVey, founder of the Church of Satan, in the essay "The Invisible War"

In August of 1996, a panel composed of Col. Tamzy J. House, Lt Col. James B. Near, Jr., LTC William B. Shields, Maj Ronald J. Celentano, Maj. David M. Husband, Maj. Ann E. Mercer, and Maj. James E. Pugh submitted a report to the U.S. Air Force entitled "Weather as a Force Multiplier: Owning the Weather in 2025." The report stated that it was "designed to comply with a directive from the chief of staff of the Air Force to examine the concepts, capabilities, and technologies the United States will require to remain the dominant air and space force in the future." This research study was quite blunt in stating one of the goals of U.S. war planners, which is to " 'own the weather' by capitalizing on emerging technologies and focusing development of those technologies to war-fighting applications. Such a technology offers the war fighter tools to shape the battlespace in ways never before possible...Weather-modification offers the war fighter a wide-range of possible options to defeat or coerce an adversary."[31]

The report goes on to note that as early as "1957, the president's advisory committee on weather control explicitly recognized the military potential of weather-modification, warning in their report that it could become a more important weapon than the atom bomb," while further warning that: "a high-risk, high-reward endeavor, weather-modification offers a dilemma not unlike the splitting of the atom. While some segments of society will always be reluctant to examine controversial issues such as weather-modification, the tremendous military capabilities that could result from this field are ignored at our own peril." One statement in particular demonstrates the devastating military power that weather-modification could yield: "The desirability to modify storms to support military objectives is the most aggressive and controversial type of weather-modification. The damage caused by storms is indeed horrendous. For instance, a tropical storm has an energy equal to 10,000 one-megaton hydrogen bombs..."[32]

The conclusion reached by the authors is that "In the United States, weather-modification will likely become a part of national security policy with both domestic and international applications."[33] This will be accomplished, it is explained, by utilizing "powerful 'ionosphere heaters' and clouds generated by chemical condensation trails—contrails—spread behind airborne tankers."[34] The ionosphere, the report informs us, is "a natural gift that humans have used to create long-range communications connecting distant points on the globe."[35] It seems only natural then that this same natural gift should be exploited to inflict suffering for military gain.

Meanwhile, in a remote region of Alaska the Pentagon has built, with little fanfare, a facility which is known as the High

Altitude Auroral Research Project, or simply as HAARP. While the Pentagon assures us this is "purely a scientific research facility which represents no threat to potential adversaries and would therefore have no value as a military target,"[36] it is unclear whether this disclaimer has resulted in any Russian missiles being re-targeted to date. What is clear is that the facility houses "an advanced model of an 'ionospheric heater.' Put simply, the apparatus for HAARP is a reversal of a radio telescope; antennas send out signals instead of receiving. HAARP is the test run for a super-powerful radiowave-beaming technology that lifts areas of the ionosphere by focusing a beam and heating those areas."[37] In other words, a turbo-charged version of the ionospheric heaters mentioned in the Air Force report.

What limited reporting there has been on the HAARP project would seem to confirm that it is indeed the type of weather-modification facility envisioned by the panel. It has been reported, for instance that "internal HAARP documents obtained through the Freedom of Information Act (FOIA) reveal that the project's goal is to 'perturb' the ionosphere with extremely powerful beams of energy and study 'how it responds to the disturbances and how it ultimately recovers,' "[38] and that "U.S. military documents put it more clearly—HAARP aims to learn how to 'exploit the ionosphere for Department of Defense purposes.' "[39] From this, one might be tempted to think that the military has already set about achieving their goal to "own the weather."

Some might even begin to wonder whether such tinkering with the ionosphere might help explain why "this winter has produced some of the wackiest weather ever seen over the United States. Usually a hot-weather phenomenon, dozens of wintertime tornadoes have struck Arkansas, Tennessee, Louisiana and Alabama this year. On February 11–12, temperatures in Chicago, Dayton, Charleston, Indianapolis and other cities ricocheted between the low seventies and the twenties, with overnight snow falling in some of those cities basking in sunlight during the day. While temperature records are normally broken by no more than a tenth of a degree, the World Meteorological Organization reports global temperatures up more than 0.6 degrees Celsius since the end of the last century. As Pacific hurricanes packing 220 mile-per-hour winds introduce a new Category 6 into storm lexicons, tropical mahi mahi and marlin are being caught off the coast of Washington state. Department of Energy researchers Alan Schroeder and David Bassett note that 15 weather-related disasters in the U.S. since 1992 have cost $70 billion in damages and several hundred deaths from floods, heat waves, hurricanes, blizzards and hail storms."[40]

Aside from its weather modification capabilities, it appears that the HAARP project may have other military functions as well, making it a true multi-use facility. Some of these uses are spelled out in the primary patent under which the HAARP site is believed to have been built: "By appropriate application of various aspects of this invention at strategic locations and with adequate power sources, a means and method is provided to cause interference with or even total disruption of communications over a very large portion of earth...This would have significant military implications, particularly as a barrier to or confusing factor for hostile missions or airplanes...

"This invention has a phenomenal variety of possible ramifications and potential future developments. As alluded to earlier, missile or aircraft destruction, deflection, or confusion could result, particularly when relativistic particles are employed. Also, large regions of the atmosphere could be lifted to an unexpectedly high altitude so that missiles encounter unexpected and unplanned drag forces with resultant destruction or deflection of same." In regards to the "strategic locations with adequate power sources," the patent notes that "Alaska provides easy access to magnetic field lines that are especially suited to the practice of this invention, since many field lines which extend to desirable altitudes for this invention intersect the earth in Alaska. Thus, in Alaska, there is a unique combination of large, accessible fuel sources at desirable field line intersections."[41]

Another of the "phenomenal variety" of uses for HAARP was revealed on June 14, 1995, when "a Senate committee report noted that the Deputy Secretary of Defense had called for increasing HAARP funding from $5 million to $75 million in the 1996 defense budget. The sudden increase would be used to promote a disturbing new mission for HAARP. Instead of just pouring its vast energy into the skies, the transmitter's power would be aimed back at the planet to 'allow earth-penetrating tomography over most of the northern hemisphere'—in effect turning HAARP into the world's most powerful 'X-ray machine' capable of scanning regions hidden deep beneath the planet's surface."[42] While the government maintains that the utilization of HAARP in this way is for the purpose of locating such things as underground bunkers, weapons factories and arms depots, a considerable amount of evidence indicates that this same technology can be used for far more controversial purposes. As researchers Nick Begich and Jeane Manning recount:

> Air Force documents revealed that a system had been developed for maintaining and disrupting human mental processes through pulsed radio-frequency radiation (the stuff of HAARP) over large geographical areas. The most telling material about this technology came from writings of Zbigniew Brzezinski (former National Security Advisor to U.S. President Carter) and J.F. MacDonald (science advisor to U.S. President Johnson and a professor of Geophysics at UCLA), as they wrote about use of power-beaming transmitters for geophysical and environmental warfare... The following statement was made more than twenty-five years ago, in a book by Brzezinski which he wrote while a professor at Columbia University:
>
> > Political strategists are tempted to exploit research on the brain and human behavior. Geophysicist Gordon J.F. MacDonald—specialist in problems of warfare—says accurately-timed, artificially-excited electronic strokes "could lead to a pattern of oscillations that produce relatively high power levels over certain regions of the earth...In this way, one could develop a system that would seriously impair the brain performance of very large populations in selected regions over an extended period"...No matter how deeply disturbing the thought of using the environment to manipulate behavior for national advantages, to some, the technology permitting such use will very probably develop within the next few decades.
>
> ...As early as 1970, Zbigniew Brzezinski predicted a "more controlled and directed society" would gradually appear, linked to tech-

nology…"Unhindered by restraints of traditional liberal values, this elite would not hesitate to achieve its political ends by using the latest modern techniques for influencing public behavior and keeping society under close surveillance and control. Technical and scientific momentum would then feed on the situation it exploits," Brzezinski predicted.

…In another document prepared by the government, the U.S. Air Force claims:

> The potential applications of artificial electromagnetic fields are wide-ranging and can be used in many military or quasi-military situations…Some of these potential uses include dealing with terrorist groups, crowd control, controlling breaches of security at military installations, and antipersonnel techniques in tactical warfare. In all of these cases the EM (electromagnetic) systems would be used to produce mild to severe physiological disruption or perceptual distortion or disorientation. In addition, the ability of individuals to function could be degraded to such a point that they would be combat ineffective. Another advantage of electromagnetic systems is that they can provide coverage over large areas with a single system. They are silent and countermeasures to them may be difficult to develop.[43]

In addition to HAARP, various other manifestations of this EM technology are believed to be either in existence or in development U.S. News has reported, for example, that "weapons already exist that use lasers, which can temporarily or permanently blind enemy soldiers. So-called acoustic or sonic weapons…can vibrate the insides of humans to stun them, nauseate them, or even 'liquefy their bowels and reduce them to quivering diarrheic messes,' according to a Pentagon briefing…Other, stranger effects also have been explored, such as using electromagnetic waves to put human targets to sleep or to heat them up, on the microwave-oven principle. Scientists are also trying to make a sonic cannon that throws a shock wave with enough force to knock down a man."[44] All such weaponry is generally referred to only under the disinformational euphemism of "non-lethal technology." In chapter 2, it was revealed that the U.S. stood alone in the world community on the issues of prohibiting the expansion of the arms race into space and banning the development of new types of weapons of mass destruction. In the previous chapter, the reason for America's opposition to the former was revealed. Perhaps the High Altitude Auroral Research Project played a key role in opposition to the latter.

For a more in-depth look at HAARP and related technology, see:

Nick Begich and Jeane Manning, *Angels Don't Play This HAARP*: Advances in *Tesla Technology*.

Kosovo—The Sacrificial Lamb?

Our mission in Kosovo has nothing to do with trying to acquire territory or dominate others.

— President Bill Clinton, Speaking at Spangdahlem Air Base, Germany, May 5, 1999

April, 1999

As the United States and its NATO allies proceed to rain indiscriminate death down upon the largely defenseless but nevertheless proud and defiant people of Yugoslavia, making it the fourth sovereign nation in the last seven months to be the recipient of a flagrantly illegal bombing campaign by the United States, the time has clearly come for the American people to take an honest and unflinching look at the course this country is currently on. This is, unfortunately, a task made extraordinarily difficult by a mainstream press that functions as the most vastly efficient propaganda machine the world has ever seen. And like all propaganda, the information flooding the U.S. airwaves is designed to preempt independent thought, dissent, or meaningful discussion. The reason for this, quite obviously, is that all of the official justifications being disseminated by administration officials, if subjected to any level of critical analysis, appear simply preposterous.

Foremost among the "official" reasons for the necessity of this bombing campaign has been the humanitarian goal of stopping the allegedly genocidal policies of the Serbian regime directed at the Albanian population of Kosovo, which have resulted in the estimated deaths of 2,000 ethnic Albanians in the past year. The United States, we are expected to believe, has suddenly developed a conscience and a concern for the human rights of oppressed minorities. Yet where was this concern just a few short years ago when a genocide of truly epic proportions was being waged against the Tutsi population of Rwanda, with the full knowledge of the United States and its UN and NATO allies? In what many consider to be one of the most brutally efficient acts of genocide ever perpetrated by man, an estimated 800,000 men, women and children were rounded up and slaughtered in just 100 days.

Adopting a decidedly non-humanitarian posture, the United States and its European allies not only failed to send in a peacekeeping force, but actually withdrew the forces already in place there, willfully allowing the savagery to proceed. This repugnant chapter of world history was notably ignored by the U.S. press as well as by the White House.* It bears noting here that it would take the Serb forces *a full 400 years*, working at their current "genocidal" pace, to match the appalling body count attained in Rwanda in just 100 days. It would take the *next four years* just to achieve the death toll reached by the Hutu death squads in a single average day. None of this is meant to downplay the tragic deaths of the Albanians, but rather to point out the stunning hypocrisy, duplicity and cynicism of a nation that would claim to wage war on their behalf, while failing to do so on behalf of the far more victimized Tutsis of Rwanda.

There are numerous other examples of oppressed ethnic minorities whose plight the United States has conspicuously ignored for decades, when not willfully contributing to their oppression, either directly or through covert actions. If the Albanians are to be granted autonomy, then shall we also now support an independent nation of Palestine, in opposition to their Israeli oppressors? And what of the Kurds? Far from supporting an independent Kurdistan, The U.S. recently arranged for the arrest—and very likely execution—of the movement's leader, Abdullah Ocalan, as well as providing long-term military support and training to Turkish forces to ensure the continuation of the Kurds' oppression, resulting to date in an estimated 35,000 Kurdish deaths, as well as hundreds of thousands being forced from their homes (560,000 according to the U.S. State Department, though other estimates run considerably higher).

Not long ago, before Saddam Hussein became America's favorite villain, we afforded the same courtesy to Iraq. Now, we merely turn a blind eye as Turk forces routinely cross the Iraqi border to decimate Kurdish villages. During the second week of NATO's bombing of the former Yugoslavia, for instance, an estimated 15,000 Turkish troops crossed the Iraqi border in the latest military attack on the Iraqi Kurds. This assault included air power in the form of U.S.-supplied Cobra attack helicopters which, by necessity, flew through the heavily patrolled, U.S.-imposed northern "no-fly zone." Astute readers will recall that the stated purpose of this illegal restriction of Iraqi airspace is specifically to protect the Kurds from this type of military attack, albeit by "bad" Iraqi troops, as opposed to "good" Turkish troops.

Closer to home, how will this new enlightened view of world affairs affect the Native American population? Shall the American Indian Movement now be allowed to secede from the union with a sizable chunk of the former United States? This hardly seems likely, any more than it does that the U.S. will decide to intervene on behalf of the Kurds, the Palestinians, the Mayans, the Tibetans or any of the world's dozens of other oppressed minorities for that matter, unless it furthers American economic and military interests to do so. The appeals to humanitarian concerns, then, seem a rather obvious and cynical attempt to manipulate public opinion. It is well worth noting here that at the United Nations Human Rights Commission's most recent annual session, Amnesty International, the most well known and widely-respected international human rights organization, placed the United States, for the first time, on its list of countries who are the world's worst violators of human rights. We now find ourselves in the elite company of such nations as Turkey, Rwanda, Congo, and Cambodia. Perhaps then it is best that we leave the job of global policeman to someone better suited to the task.

Implicit in the rhetoric of "genocide" and "ethnic cleansing" is the assumption that what is occurring is a one-sided, barbaric attack against a civilian population. Yet this is directly contradicted by statements made by top U.S. officials. The KLA, now warmly embraced as some sort of Reaganesque "freedom fighters," were only a year ago described by the U.S. State Department as "without question a terrorist group." Just two months before the bombs began to fall, CIA Director George Tenet, speaking before the Senate Armed Services Committee, said: "The Kosovo Liberation Army will emerge from the winter better trained, better equipped and better led than last year...We assess that if fighting escalates in the spring—as we expect—it will be bloodier than last year's...Both sides likely will step up attacks on civilians...The recent attacks against Serb bars and restaurants in Pristina and Pec could be the beginning of a pattern of tit-for-tat retaliation that will grow more severe as fighting intensifies."

Unstated by the CIA Director was precisely how the KLA had gotten better trained, armed and led, though Mr. Tenet's organization has been known to provide such services. Tenet did say of the KLA that it was "dedicated to overthrowing Belgrade's rule by force. The KLA grew quickly and was able last spring to mount low-level attacks against Serb police forces and expand its presence throughout the province, even exercising effective control over some areas in central Kosovo." Viewed in this context, it's interesting to speculate on what type of "ethnic cleansing" policy the U.S. might adopt towards a large secessionist group armed, trained and led by a foreign intelligence service and dedicated to the armed overthrow of U.S. rule. Though the Branch Davidians hardly qualified as such a threat, one need look no further than Waco, Texas, to see that the response would be swift and brutal.

We are also being told, as we were to justify the genocidal war with Iraq, that Serbia's leader, Slobodan Milosevic, is evil incarnate, the heir apparent to Adolph Hitler. From this we are to deduce that Milosevic is a madman bent on global imperialism and genocidal actions of horrendous proportions, and with the resources to achieve his goals. This analogy could not possibly be any more absurd. Far from presiding over an expanding power base, the Serbian regime has for the last decade watched its empire fracture and crumble. None of the Serb military actions of the last decade were aimed at expansion of the Yugoslav republic, but rather at preventing the further contraction of its borders. In fact, in 1995, several hundred thousand Serbs were themselves the victims of "ethnic cleansing," being forced from their homes by the U.S.-armed-and-trained army of Croatia. In truth, Milosevic is nothing more than the ruler of a rapidly fragmenting, militarily insignificant republic that is also notably light on industry for a would-be superpower.

There is, however, a chilling parallel with Hitler that has gone unmentioned in the U.S. press. In 1938, Nazi Germany invaded Czechoslovakia for the allegedly purely humanitarian aim of ending ethnic violence in the Sudenten region of the country. Conveniently left out of this justification was the fact that the Nazis had actively encouraged an uprising in that area for the express purpose of using the repression of that movement by Czech forces as a pretext for the military intervention. We might also note here that Nazi Germany was the last imperialist power to dump bombs down upon the Serbian capital of Belgrade.

As further justification for the U.S. offensive, the American people have been told repeatedly that it is imperative for the continued credibility of NATO that this action be taken. Indeed, our commitment to NATO requires that this action be taken, or so we have been led to believe. Nothing, however, could be further from the truth. NATO was established as, and for 50 years has functioned as, a specifically *defensive* alliance. NATO was founded for the express purpose of defending member nations from acts of foreign aggression, particularly by the former Soviet Union. No longer having an evil empire to defend itself from, the NATO alliance has found a new purpose in life—humanitarian bombing. This despite the fact that Serbia has not conducted or even threatened any acts of aggression against any NATO member, or against any sovereign nation for that matter.

Far from being actions taken to ensure the continued relevance of NATO, these acts of war being perpetrated against the Serbian people are a deliberate attempt to rewrite the NATO charter, which is quite obviously one of the true goals of this intervention. The

U.S. clearly sees NATO as an organization which can be more easily manipulated to serve the cynical goals of the White House than can the UN. The U.S. would apparently like to see the authority of the UN usurped by NATO, thereby relieving Washington of the need to seek a more broad-based international consensus before launching offensive military actions. It should be noted here that it is the UN, and only the UN, that is authorized by international law to sanction the use of force. NATO has no such legal authority, making the current air war, conducted without UN Security Council approval, a clear violation of international law.

At any rate, the notion that this is a NATO action is largely an illusion. Just as in the Gulf War, the appearance of an international alliance is essentially a fig leaf aimed at legitimizing U.S. acts of aggression in the eyes of the American public and the world community. Reporters on the scene in the Balkans during the first week of bombings have noted that 84% of the sorties being flown are by American pilots. NATO itself has reported that, including the cruise missiles being launched from U.S. warships, fully 90% of the raw tonnage of explosives being unleashed on Yugoslavia is of U.S. origin, meaning that the other eighteen countries in the alliance are contributing roughly 1/2 of 1% of the firepower each, on average.

There are, to be sure, other U.S. goals being pursued in the Balkans. One of these is to provide additional justification for greatly increasing the U.S. military budget, already grotesquely bloated by any sane reasoning. It was not many years ago that military increases were being justified on the grounds that America must be prepared to fight two regional wars simultaneously. This situation has already, not surprisingly, come to pass, as the U.S. currently conducts overt acts of war against two sovereign nations, Serbia and Iraq. There is little doubt that we will next be told that we need to up the ante further yet, perhaps to ensure the preparedness of the U.S. military to fight three concurrent wars, as more and more money is pumped into the U.S. war machine, already far and away the greatest merchant of death in the modern world.

Hidden deep beneath the rhetoric of U.S. policy makers lurk far more ominous U.S. goals in the Balkan crisis. Well known among State Department and intelligence personnel, though not among the American people, is the U.S. desire to unleash the power of tactical nuclear weaponry upon the world. The White House has been trying for some time now, unsuccessfully, to set up a pretext to use these weapons against the Hussein regime in Iraq. Repeated and sustained bombing missions, occurring sometimes daily, though virtually ignored by the U.S. press, have been intended to provoke attacks by Iraqi forces on the Turkish and Saudi air bases from which these "sorties" are being flown. Though Iraq would be arguably justified by international law in launching such attacks, for the legitimate purpose of acting in its own self-defense, the U.S. could quickly seize upon such an occurrence to escalate the war to a nuclear level. After all, it could be argued, if Hussein were to proceed to launch "unprovoked" attacks against its neighbors, despite eight years of aerial bombardment and the imposition of the harshest possible economic sanctions, what else is a "peacekeeper" to do?

Frustratingly for U.S. officials, Hussein has stubbornly refused to take the bait, despite occasional threats to do so. And so it is entirely possible that the U.S. has shifted its nuclear testing grounds to Serbia. The most likely pretext here would be the necessity of stopping the Albanian "genocide," presumably at any cost. Already we are told that air power alone will not achieve this goal. Ground forces could prove effective, we are assured, though this is a politically unpopular option, and mobilization of a sufficient force would take a considerable amount of time, during which the "ethnic cleansing" will continue. The solution here seems terrifyingly obvious—use the threat of, and indeed the actual deployment of, tactical nuclear weapons to force the withdrawal of Serbian troops from Kosovo. The world's first humanitarian use of nuclear weapons.

There is also the very real possibility that Washington will decide against the nuclear option (perhaps saving that honor for North Korea, though Iraq remains a strong contender), choosing instead to deploy ground forces. Pursuing this option could conceivably enable the military establishment to attain yet another unspoken goal—the resumption of the draft. The military has made no secret of late of its desire to greatly increase manpower. There have been grave warnings of the imminent danger we face if military manpower is not increased, these coming even before the onset of the current war. There can be little doubt that the deployment of ground troops to Kosovo would provoke immediate calls for a military draft. In the ongoing campaign to militarize the country, reinstatement of military conscription is clearly a necessary component.

Already I can hear the protests from my fellow Americans, asserting that the United States would not embark on such courses of action unless forced to. The conventional wisdom states that the U.S. uses its military might only when forced to by others, and only in defense of cherished democratic principles. For example, while it is undeniably true that America stands alone in the unconscionable use of atomic weaponry, against civilian population centers no less, our history books tell us it was done only to avoid even greater carnage than the 250,000 or more lives lost in Hiroshima and Nagasaki. This explanation is dubious, at best, and certainly does little to explain the use of conventional weaponry to rain mass carnage upon numerous German and Japanese population centers during our involvement in World War II prior to dropping the atom bombs.

Are we to believe that the U.S. had no other option than to firebomb the city of Dresden, Germany, resulting in an estimated 130,000 civilian deaths in a single sustained bombing raid? Or that a similar attack upon Tokyo that killed 80,000 civilians was in legitimate pursuit of promoting democratic principles? Was America, in fact, forced to incinerate most major German and Japanese cities in order to save them, to such an extent that U.S. military planners fretted that there would be no unfazed areas of Japan left in which to test the atomic bombs? While much has been made of the deplorable conduct of the German Luftwaffe during WWII, the equally appalling actions of the U.S. Air Force, as well as the British RAF, have remained largely unquestioned, though American and Allied air power was responsible for more civilian deaths than was German air power.

The targeting of civilians by American forces was not a situation unique to World War II, by any means. It has, in fact, been an integral part of U.S. military policy for quite some time. A full century ago, beginning in 1899, the United States waged a savage war in the Philippines, decimating countless Philippine villages and their inhabitants because, according to President McKinley, "they were unfit for self-government." In this act of military aggression, missing from most American history texts and therefore unknown to virtually all Americans, the policy adopted by General Smith was to kill "everything over [the age of] ten." That the barbarism was of such an extreme degree is exemplified by the statement of General Shafter, the U.S. Field Commander, who said: "It may be necessary to kill half the Filipinos in order that the remaining half of the population may be advanced to a higher plane of life." In the U.S. Congress, the action was justified by Senator Albert Beveridge, among others, who pointed out that: "Senators must remember that we are not dealing with Americans or Europeans. We are dealing with Orientals."

In strikingly similar actions taken against Korea in the 1950s, and Vietnam in the 1960s and 1970s, we would again be dealing with "Orientals," and with appallingly similar results. The total number of Asian deaths directly attributable to U.S. military actions in these three undeclared wars could be as high as five million or more, including the hundreds of thousands of Cambodian and Laotian victims of Nixon's "secret" bombings of those countries concurrent with the Vietnam War. It was not until Vietnam that the true horror of these Asian military interventions began to come to light, with revelations of entire villages being burned and their civilian inhabitants summarily executed, most notoriously at the village of My Lai, where hundreds of villagers were lined up in irrigation ditches and shredded with automatic weapon fire. In these arguably genocidal wars, indiscriminate death was showered upon civilians and military personnel alike, not only with conventional weaponry, but with chemical agents such as napalm, agent orange and white phosphorous incendiary devices. Though the U.S. stubbornly refuses to classify these as chemical weapons, by any rational analysis they clearly fall into that category.

Depleted-uranium weapons, used extensively in the war against Iraq, and now against Serbia, should also be classified as chemical weapons, and could arguably even be considered low grade nuclear weapons, due to their nasty habit of leaving a cloud of radioactive residue scattered throughout the area of bombardment. By U.S. reckoning, however, these are merely conventional weapons. So are the truly repugnant cluster bombs and fuel-air bombs which were also dropped with impunity against the people of Iraq, to complement the generous quantities of napalm. What all of these weapons share is the ability to keep on killing long after the hostilities have ended. Depleted uranium, agent orange, and napalm all cause lasting environmental damage and pose major health risks that last for generations. Cluster bombs, on the other hand, have a bad habit of leaving a large number of unexploded "bomblets" laying about. In Southeast Asia people are, to this day, killed or injured by American cluster bomblets more than a quarter century since the last bombs were dropped.

This brief and by no means exhaustive review of U.S. military history in the twentieth century is presented here to emphasize the fact that America is no stranger to the use of weapons of mass destruction, nor to the use of conventional weapons in such a way as to insure massive numbers of civilian casualties. America is also intimately familiar with the notion of "ethnic cleansing," having enthusiastically contributed, along with the European colonial powers, to the most thorough act of ethnic cleansing ever perpetrated by man, the systematic eradication of tens of millions of Native Americans from throughout the Americas. Even today we continue in that fine tradition, having recently admitted to our complicity in the slaughter of 200,000 Mayan Indians in Guatemala in the previous two decades. Another form of ethnic cleansing occurs within our borders today, cynically disguised as the "war on drugs," though it would more accurately be described as a war on undesirables, with most of its victims being blacks and hispanics. It is hard to see how expelling people from their homes and homelands, as cruel as this is, constitutes any more of an inhumane act than criminalizing an entire generation of young "ethnic" Africans, and imprisoning them in increasingly barbaric conditions, where many will be denied their freedom for the rest of their lives.

Yet all this sordid recent history does not fully explain the repugnant level of militarism and belligerent nationalism currently on display in this country. It does not explain, for instance, the surreal casualness with which this country now enters into military interventions, dispensing with any level of public or congressional debate. Nor does it explain why the U.S. would turn, at this point in history, to the use of tactical nuclear weapons or to the resumption of a military draft. For this we need to look at the current state of the global and U.S. economies.

The truth is that the current system of global free market capitalism is failing, though the American press, dazzled by the dizzying heights reached by the venerated Dow Jones, would have us believe quite the opposite. In Russia, for example, the economic distress among the people is at a level unmatched in the darkest days of "communist" rule. In other countries as well, in Asia and South America, the system is nearly on the verge of collapse. Around the world, cracks and fissures are appearing everywhere. In the United States, the economy is widely perceived as being abundantly healthy, one of the saving graces of the Clinton administration. This is largely an illusion created by the fixation on the Dow Jones industrial average as the key indicator of economic health. Far from being an indicator of the overall health of the country, however, it would be more accurate to view it as an indicator of the severe polarization of wealth that characterizes America today. Never before has so much wealth been concentrated in so few hands.

The already massive gap between rich and poor grows larger with each corporate merger, with each company downsizing. Deskilling of the labor force can be seen at work everywhere, transforming stable, high paying jobs into unskilled positions in which low paid workers are readily interchangeable. The American middle class, the traditional buffer zone between the wealthy and the desperately poor, is rapidly disappearing. And with it have gone many of the traditional safety nets that have sustained Americans through hard times, such as welfare and affordable health care. Social Security and Medicare will fare no better in the hands of those who would claim to be "fixing" them.

The reality yet to be faced by the American people is that the bubble of apparent economic prosperity we are currently living in cannot be sustained forever. The bubble will soon burst, as it has elsewhere, bringing massive layoffs and suffering for the working people of America. Americans will soon learn that the safety nets and social programs whose decimation they supported, conned by the racist sloganeering of cynical politicians, were intended for the benefit of *all* Americans. And they will also learn that, faced with extreme economic despair and seething anger among the people, and lacking an effective buffer zone, the moneyed elite will be compelled to resort to massive levels of force to maintain their hold on their grossly disproportionate share of the world's wealth.

The U.S. corporate and military interests, being the primary architects of the current global system, are not about to lose control of that system, a message that is being sent every time the U.S. military flexes its considerable muscle. America has made quite clear its intention to use whatever means necessary to prop up the system. It is precisely in this context that we could well see the U.S. unleash tactical nuclear weapons in either the Iraqi or the Serbian interventions. The need to project this military resolve to the world, particularly those "rogue" nations resistant to U.S. hegemony, is also why we will very likely also see the restoration of the draft in the foreseeable future.

On the domestic front, Washington is well aware of the anger and rebellion that will accompany large scale unemployment with little, if any, meaningful government relief remaining. Washington is also well aware of the resistance that could accompany the reinstatement of the draft. This is why we see the prison population already rising to astoundingly high levels, while the building of new prisons is one of the largest growth industries in the country. More ominously, we see the rise in private prison construction and management, and the use of prison labor by hugely profitable corporations at third world labor rates. Meanwhile, the use of the death penalty spirals out of control, claiming among its victims women, the mentally retarded, and even those committing crimes as minors.

In other ways as well, the line dividing juvenile crime from adult crime has been all but eliminated. In the name of fighting the war on drugs, we have allowed the increasing militarization of our police forces, tolerated a rising tide of police abuse, and allowed the rise of the prosecutorial police state and watched in silence as it ran roughshod over our most cherished constitutional protections. Not content with the speed with which the war on drugs was usurping our rights, we welcomed with open arms the equally reactionary war

215

on terrorism, with its goal of merging the various levels of local, state and federal police into a single, unified "anti-terrorist" paramilitary force. In doing so, we have laid the groundwork for the most extreme levels of oppressive force imaginable.

These trends are not appearing only in the U.S., of course, but rather are mirrored, to varying degrees, throughout the Western world. But it is only in America that there is such an obscene concentration of the world's wealth. And it is only in America, land of the grotesquely bloated military budget, that the firepower exists to enforce one country's agenda on an international level. And so it is that while the sheep lie sleeping, falsely secure in their belief that their constitutional protections are "inalienable rights," the march towards global techno-fascism proceeds. Best of luck in the New World Order.

For a harrowing look at the Rwandan genocide and the U.S. response at the time, see "The Triumph of Evil" PBS Frontline.

ON LITTLETON AND RAMBOUILLET

On April 20, in the wake of the Littleton tragedy, President Clinton told the country, seemingly without a trace of irony, that "we must reach out to our children and teach them to express their anger and to resolve their conflicts with words, not weapons." The president appeared to be unaware that the example he sets for the children is more a product of his actions than of the self-serving and sanctimonious words he offered to the nation. It is important then to understand the extent to which the U.S. attempted to resolve the Kosovo matter "with words, not weapons."

As any American who has watched the TV news or read a newspaper is aware, the diplomatic process was thwarted by Milosevic's stubborn refusal to accept a peaceful solution aimed only at protecting the Albanian Kosovars. The terms of the agreement, as presented to the American people by the media, seem entirely reasonable.

Clearly the United States made a good faith effort to avoid the use of force, an effort that should have succeeded had Milosevic been a more reasonable leader. We know all this because it is universally agreed upon by the entire mainstream media apparatus. But is it true?

One has only to read the Rambouillet Accord, specifically Appendix B, to see that the demands made upon Serbia by the NATO delegates were so patently absurd as to virtually guarantee that the document would be rejected, which it was—though by the Serbian Parliament and not Milosevic personally. It would, in fact, have been rejected by any sovereign nation on earth. For contrary to what is commonly believed, the Rambouillet Accord would have required the surrender of the *entire* Federal Republic of Yugoslavia to foreign military occupation and rule. This offer was non-negotiable. The only alternative was massive aerial destruction. It would appear that if our children are choosing to resolve their conflicts with weapons rather than words, they are merely showing the true face of America.

"NATO personnel shall enjoy, together with their vehicles, vessels, aircraft, and equipment, free and unrestricted passage and unimpeded access throughout the FRY [Federal Republic of Yugoslavia] including associated airspace and territorial waters. This shall include, but not be limited to, the right of bivouac, maneuver, billet, and utilization of any areas or facilities as required for support, training, and operations...NATO shall be immune from all legal process, whether civil, administrative, or criminal...NATO personnel, under all circumstances and at all times, shall be immune from the Parties, jurisdiction in respect of any civil, administrative, criminal, or disciplinary offenses which may be committed by them in the FRY...NATO personnel shall be immune from any form of arrest, investigation, or detention by the authorities in the FRY...NATO shall be exempt from duties, taxes, and other charges and inspections and custom regulations including providing inventories or other routine customs documentation, for personnel, vehicles, vessels, aircraft, equipment, supplies, and provisions entering, exiting, or transiting the territory of the FRY in support of the operation...The authorities in the FRY shall facilitate, on a priority basis and with all appropriate means, all movement of personnel, vehicles, vessels, aircraft, equipment, or supplies, through or in the airspace, ports, airports, or roads used...Vehicles, vessels, and aircraft used in support of the operation shall not be subject to licensing or registration requirements, nor commercial insurance...and the right to use all of the electromagnetic spectrum for this purpose, free of cost...The Parties shall provide, free of cost, such public facilities as NATO shall require to prepare for and execute the operation...NATO and NATO personnel shall be immune from claims of any sort which arise out of activities in pursuance of the operation."

Interim Agreement for Peace and Self-Government in Kosovo, Appendix B: Status of Multi National Military Implementation Force, Articles 6,7,8,9,10,15,16 & 17, February 23, 1999

THE *NEW YORK TIMES* AND IDENTIFYING THE GOOD GUYS AND THE BAD GUYS

The following excerpts come from a 1987 *New York Times* article. The strong bias of the article, which today would be denounced as pro-Serb propaganda, stands in stark contrast to the current demonization of Serbia by the mainstream media, clearly showing the eagerness of the American media to shape the "news" to conform to shifting U.S. goals:

"Ethnic Albanians in the government have manipulated public funds and regulations to take over land belonging to Serbs...Slavic Orthodox churches have been attacked, and flags have been torn down. Wells have been poisoned and crops burned. Slavic boys have been knifed, and some young ethnic Albanians have been told by their elders to rape Serbian girls...The principal battleground is the region called Kosovo...As Slavs flee the protracted violence, Kosovo is becoming what ethnic Albanian nationalists have been demanding for years, and especially strongly since the bloody rioting by ethnic Albanians in Pristina in 1981—an 'ethnically pure' Albanian region, a 'Republic of Kosovo' in all but name...Were the ethnic tensions restricted to Kosovo, Yugoslavia's problems with its Albanian nationals might be more manageable...The federal Secretary for National Defense, Fleet Adm. Branko Mamula, told the army's party organization in September of efforts by ethnic Albanians to subvert the armed forces...Ethnic Albanians already control almost every phase of life in the autonomous province of Kosovo, including the police, judiciary, schools and factories."

New York Times, November 1, 1987

As the next excerpt shows, as recently as June of 1998 the *Times* was still slanting its coverage of Kosovo in favor of the Serbs. The good guys and bad guys would soon be changing places:

"In recent days the rebels have changed their strategy and begun to attack and kidnap Serbian civilians in an apparent effort to drive them out of their villages in the overwhelmingly Albanian province of Kosovo in Southern Serbia...Armed ethnic Albanian groups have expelled Serbs from Jelovac and Kijevo...and several say male relatives detained by the rebels are still missing ... Bodies have begun turning up near Serbian settlements. Zivojin Milic, shot six times in the head, was found last Wednesday on the outskirts of Pristina, apparently a victim of the ethnic Albanian militants."

New York Times, June 24, 1998

Acknowledgments

First and foremost, my profound thanks to everyone at Common Courage Press, particularly to Greg Bates, whose editing, advice and guidance proved invaluable, though not always initially well received. Special thanks also goes to Arthur Stamoulis for his typesetting skills, Kris Lamoreau for her marketing savvy, and Erica Bjerning for her fantastic cover design.

My sincerest thanks also go to the many fine organizations whose research and reports on those issues which the mainstream media choose to ignore inspired and facilitated my own research. Though none of these groups were directly involved in the creation of this book, the excerpts taken from their unparalleled investigative reports provide the backbone for many of the chapters herein. These groups are, in alphabetical order:

The British American Security Information Council; the Death Penalty Information Center; the Electronic Privacy Information Center; Fairness and Accuracy in Reporting; the Historical Clarification Commission; Human Rights Watch; the International Action Center; the International Federation of Red Cross and Red Crescent Societies; the Justice Policy Institute; the National Criminal Justice Commission; Privacy International; Project Censored; UNICEF; the United Nations Development Program, Environmental Program, and Food and Agricultural Organization; and the World Health Organization.

Last, but certainly not least, a very special thanks goes to Amnesty International, whose prominence in several chapters of this book is testament both to the quality and thoroughness of their reporting, and to the lack thereof by the corporate media.

Notes

1   *Los Angeles Times*, March 14, 1996
2   Associated Press, January 11, 1999
3   BBC News "UN Warns of Earth Crisis," September 15, 1999
4   Ibid
5   BBC News "First Cloned Human Embryo Revealed," June 17, 1999
6   BBC News "Human Cloning Experiments Underway," June 17, 1999
7   BBC News "First Cloned Human Embryo Revealed," June 17, 1999
8   The U.S. Human Genome Project Website
9   Environmental News Network "Is Your Breakfast Genetically Engineered?" September 28, 1998
10 Ibid
11 BBC News "U.S. Farmers Fear GM Crop Fallout," July 14, 1999
12 Environmental News Network "Is Your Breakfast Genetically Engineered?" September 28, 1998
13 Val Giddings, Vice President of Biotechnology Industry Organisation, featured on *CounterPunch* website
14 BBC News "Fluorescent GM Potatoes Say 'Water Me,'" September 14, 1999
15 *The Mojo Wire* "A Seedy Business," April 7, 1998
16 Ibid
17 Ibid
18 Ibid
19 Ibid (emphasis added)
20 *Covert Action Quarterly* #33, Winter 1990
21 Ibid
22 Ibid
23 Ibid
24 *Miami Herald* "Reagan Advisers Ran Secret Government," July 5, 1987
25 Ibid
26 Ibid
27 *Covert Action Quarterly* #33, Winter 1990
28 *Miami Herald* "Reagan Advisers Ran Secret Government," July 5, 1987
29 *Covert Action Quarterly* #33, Winter 1990
30 Senate Report #93-549, entered into the congressional record in 1973
31 "Weather as a Force Multiplier: Owning the Weather in 2025," a research paper presented to Air Force 2025 by Col. Tamzy J. House, Lt. Col. James B. Near, Jr., LTC William B. Shields, Maj. Ronald J. Celentano, Maj. David M. Husband, Maj. Ann E. Mercer, Maj. James E. Pugh, August 1996
32 Ibid
33 Ibid
34 Environment News Service "Fixing the Weather," February 22, 1999
35 "Weather as a Force Multiplier: Owning the Weather in 2025," Col. Tamzy J. House, et al
36 HAARP "Fact Sheet," released to the public in November 1993
37 Dr. Nick Begich and Jeane Manning "Vandalism in the Sky," *Nexus Magazine*, December 1995–January 1996
38 Gar Smith and Clare Zichuhr "Project HAARP: The Military's Plan to Alter the Ionosphere," *Earth Island Journal*, Fall 1994
39 Dr. Nick Begich and Jeane Manning "Vandalism In The Sky," *Nexus Magazine*, December 1995–January 1996
40 Environment News Service "Fixing the Weather," February 22, 1999
41 U.S. Patent 4,686,605; August 11, 1987; Bernard J. Eastlund, inventor
42 Gar Smith and Clare Zichuhr "Project HAARP: The Military's Plan to Alter the Ionosphere," *Earth Island Journal*, Fall 1994
43 Dr. Nick Begich and Jeane Manning "Vandalism in the Sky," *Nexus Magazine*, December 1995–January 1996
44 Douglas Pasternak "Wonder Weapons," *U.S. News Online*, July 7, 1997

Source Index

Subject Index

233

About the Author

Dave McGowan grew up in Southern California where he studied sociology and psychology at UCLA, obtaining a degree in the latter. For the last ten years he has worked as a general contractor throughout the greater Los Angeles area. He currently resides in the San Fernando Valley, where he is researching yet more government malfeasance for his next book. Dave is also an avid landscape photographer who hopes to someday publish his photographic work. He can be contacted through his web site at www.davesweb.cnchost.com.